CHEFMAN DIGITAL AIR FRYER COOKBOOK FOR BEGINNERS

1200 DAYS EFFORTLESS AND DELICIOUS AIR FRYER RECIPES FOR BEGINNERS AND ADVANCED USERS

DANIEL NOLAN

Copyright©2023 Daniel Nolan
All rights reserved. No part of this book may be reproduced or used in any manner without the prior written permission of the copyright owner, except for the use of brief quotations in a book review.
First paperback edition May 2023.
Cover art by Natalie M. Kern
Printed by Amazon in the USA.
Disclaimer : Although the author and publisher have made every effort to ensure that the information in this book was correct at press time, the author and publisher do not assume and hereby disclaim any liability to any party for any loss, damage, or disruption caused by errors or omissions, whether such errors or omissions result from negligence, accident, or any other cause. this book is not intended as a substitute for the medical advice of physicians.

CONTENTS

INTRODUCTION 5

POULTRY RECIPES 10

Chicken Taco Poblano Rice Bowls 11	Bbq Chicken Wings Cooking In Air Fryer................16
Leftover Turkey Pot Pie Empanadas....................12	Air Fryer Chicken Breast 17
Air Fryer Taquitos 13	Air Fryer Chicken Milanese With Arugula...............18
Air Fryer Roast Chicken 13	Air Fryer Frozen Chicken Nuggets 18
Air Fryer Bbq Chicken Drumsticks 14	Air Fryer Asian Whole Roasted Chicken.................19
Air Fryer Turkey Legs 15	Simple Chicken Breasts...19
Air-fryer Chicken Wings With Buffalo Sauce..........15	Air Fryer Chimichangas..20
Air Fryer Chicken Thighs 16	

FISH & SEAFOOD RECIPES..21

Air Fryer Fish Tacos 22	Easy Air Fryer Lemon Garlic Salmon Recipe...........28
Crispy Air Fryer Shrimp 23	Air Fryer Miso-ginger Salmon Recipe......................29
Air Fryer Fish Cakes 24	Air Fryer Lemon & Garlic Tuna Steak......................30
Air Fryer Salmon Cakes...25	Air Fryer Salmon With Dill 30
Air Fryer Fish & Chips 26	Air Fryer Scalloped Potatoes 31
Air Fryer Low Country Boil 27	Air Fryer Beer Battered Fish Tacos 32
Air Fryer Scallops With Lemon Cream Sauce..........27	Air Fryer Cod 32
Seafood Boil In The Steam Air Fryer 28	

BEEF, PORK & LAMB RECIPES..33

Air Fryer Lamb Loin Chops With Chimichurri Sauce 34	Air-fryer Scotch Eggs..37
Air Fryer Italian Pork Chops Parmigiana 35	Air Fryer Steak..38
Prosciutto Wrapped Figs With Blue Cheese 36	Air Fryer Pork Chops 38
Grilled Watermelon Steaks 36	Air Fryer Steak Bites...39
Best Damn Air Fryer Pork Tenderloin 37	Air Fryer Boneless Pork Chops 40

BREAKFAST & BRUNCH RECIPES 41

Air-fryer Falafel Wraps Recipe..................................42	Air Fryer Falafel..45
Breakfast Sliders 43	Air Fryer Taco Shells..46
Air Fryer,herb Butter Dinner Rolls 43	Texas Toast In The Air Fryer......................................46
Air-fryer Scones..44	Air-fryer Breakfast Burritos 47
Air Fryer Breakfast Potatoes 44	Air-fryer Garlic Bread..47

DESSERTS RECIPES 48

Air-fryer Healthier Apple Chips 49	Baked Corn And Crab Cakes 50
Air Fryer Apple Crumble 49	Air Fryer Lava Cakes 51
Air Fryer Apricot And Raisin Cake............................50	Air Fryer Cheesecake Recipe....................................52

Air Fried Mac N Cheese Balls 53
Air Fryer Frozen Waffles 53
Italian Pastries With Creamy Semolina Filling 54
Fried Oreos 54

DESSERTS RECIPES 55

Air Fryer Wontons...56
Roasted Green Beans..56
Jicama Fries In The Air Fryer 57
Frozen Onion Rings In Air Fryer 57
Air Fryer Greek Crescent Nachos............................58
Air Fryer Pasta Chips...59
Air Fryer Zucchini Chips 60
Air Fryer Kale Chips 61
Poutine 61
Air Fryer Green Beans 62

FAVORITE AIR FRYER RECIPES 63

Air Fryer Fried Ravioli On A Stick 64
Air Fryer Taquitos Recipe 65
Air Fryer Sausage Crescent Cheese Balls 66
Air Fryer Mozzarella Sticks 67
Air Fryer Halloween Mummy Dogs 68
Air Fryer Pizza 69
Toasted Ravioli..70
Air Fryer English Muffin Pizzas 71
Air-fryer Jalapeño Poppers 72
Air Fryer Sausage..73

VEGETABLE & & VEGETARIAN RECIPES 74

Crispy Air Fryer Brussels Sprouts 75
Smokey Cheese & Caramelized Onion Potato Bake.76
Air Fryer Squash...77
Air-fryer Green Tomato Blt 78
Air Fryer Pickles 79
Air Fryer Squash And Zucchini 80
Air Fryer Mushrooms 81
Air-fryer Asian Bbq Cauliflower Wing Recipe 82
Air Fryer Sweet And Sour Veggies 83
Air Fryer Jacket Potato...84

SALADS & SIDE DISHES RECIPES 85

Air Fryer Burst Tomato Burrata Caprese Salad.......86
Air Fryer Roasted Garlic..87
Air Fryer Parmesan Brussel Sprouts 88
Sweet Potato Wedges With Cilantro Lime Crema ...89
Crispy Tofu With Palm Sugar Dressing In The Air Fryer..90
Air Fryer Italian Sausage With Peppers And Onions 91
Hummus-filled Portobellos With Olive Tapenade...92
Grilled Corn Salad 93
Air Fryer Salmon With Warm Potato Salad............94
Air Fryer Vietnamese-style Spring Roll Salad 95

SANDWICHES & BURGERS RECIPES 96

Air Fryer Hamburgers Recipe 97
Air-fryer Greek Turkey Burgers 98
Air Fryer Frozen Beyond Burgers® 99
Air Fryer Bacon Cheeseburger Biscuit Bombs........100
Air Fryer Hamburgers 101
Halloumi Burger...102
Fish Finger Sandwich 103
Halloumi Burger...104
Fish Finger Sandwich 105
Air Fryer Turkey Burgers 106
Air Fryer Butter Bacon Burgers 107
Low-carb Lettuce Wrap Burgers 108

INTRODACTION

Air fryers simulate the traditional frying of foods by circulating hot air around food rather than submerging the food in oil. As with frying, properly prepared foods are crispy, juicy, golden brown, and flavorful. Air fryers work due to the Maillard reaction, a scientific principle which refers to what we usually call "browning." A Maillard reaction occurs when the surface of a food item forms a crust due to dehydration, and the intense heat breaks down proteins, starches, and fibers. That is what gives fried, roasted, and baked foods their delicious, complex flavors. Air fryers employ convection to rapidly and efficiently cook crisp foods. A heating element within the air fryer super-heats the air, producing natural convection currents. A fan within the appliance aids in air movement, circulating it even more rapidly. Perforations or holes in the cooking basket allow the hot air to flow freely around the food. This air movement increases heat transfer from the air to the food. Thus, your dinner gets done faster.

Benefits of an AirFryer
There are a number of reasons why so many love air fryers, among them: Healthy cooking, faster cooking, simple and easy to use, convenient clean up and air fryers are safe to operate.

HEALTH BENEFITS
Are Air Fryers Healthy? Well If you're looking to lower cholesterol or lose weight, your doctor may thank you for using an air fryer. Air fryers use around 75 percent less oil than deep fryers, providing a healthy alternative without sacrificing flavor.

Plus, unlike microwave ovens, which use a form of electromagnetic radiation called microwaves to excite water molecules, thus heating the food due to friction, air fryers do not use any form of radiation.

QUICK AND ENERGY EFFICIENT
The air fryer's small convection oven preheats and cooks more quickly than a conventional oven. You'll have tasty meals in haste, with less wait!

Also, most air fryers are energy efficient, and shorter cook times translate to less overall power usage.

SAFE AND EASY TO USE
Lacking the large oil vats of traditional deep fryers, air fryers eliminate the risk of serious burns from spilled oil. Also, air fryers are designed so that the exterior does not become dangerously hot to the touch.

Air fryers utilize simple controls, typically two knobs for cook time and temperature, or an easy to read digital display. You simply toss the food in oil (if desired), place it in the basket, and the air fryer does the rest.

CLEAN AND TIDY
The baskets and pans of most air fryers are dishwasher safe for easy cleanup. Also, the enclosed nature of the air fryer prevents the splatters and spills associated with deep frying and pan frying.

Now, we understand how much you love your air fryer and how much you love to use it and that is why you also need to remember to keep it clean.
Fryer baskets can get a little dirtier and greasier than other kitchen appliances and grease tends to cling due to continual use. So, when you think of how to clean an air fryer it might seem a scary thing to do.

Parts of an air fryer
Here you will find a list of the most common air fryer parts and accessories you can replace yourself or it can help you with the entire cooking experience.

The air fryer baking pan. Is a removable part of your air fryer that you will cook your food in.

The air fryer basket. Another one of the air fryer baking accessories is the air fryer basket. It is very similar to the baking pan, except it comes with holes inside of it.

Air frying grill pan. Very similar to the previous accessories we mentioned is the grill pan. It comes with a perforated surface which helps to create the ideal airflow while grilling your food.

Boil out fryer cleaner is a fryer cleaner that is great for cleaning and removing oils, fats, carbon, rust, etc.

Rack with skewers for air fryer. They are made of stainless steel and are dishwasher safe. You will be able to cook two different types of food, due to the two layers of racks.

Basket divider. A basket divider will allow you to cook two food types at the same time one next to each other, without them touching.

FAQS
Can I cook frozen, canned foods in an air fryer? How do I prevent my food from sticking to the basket? How do I season my canned foods before cooking? These are common questions that people have when it comes to air frying.

Can I Cook Frozen Canned Foods In An Air Fryer?
As someone who loves air frying, I often get asked if frozen; or canned foods can be cooked in an air fryer. The answer is yes!

You can cook frozen and canned foods in your air fryer with ease. Like any other food item you plan on cooking in the air fryer, it's essential to ensure you have the proper temperature and time settings set for optimal results.

One thing to remember when cooking frozen, canned foods in an air fryer is that they may take longer than non-frozen items.

Adding a few extra minutes of cooking time or using the defrost setting before cooking is recommended. Always check for doneness before eating and adjust the settings as necessary.

With these tips and tricks, you can quickly and easily cook your favorite frozen, canned foods using your trusty air fryer.

And best of all, there's no need to defrost them before placing them into the basket!

How Do I Prevent My Food From Sticking To The Basket?
A thin layer of oil is the key to preventing food from sticking to the basket. Invest in a kitchen spray bottle and fill it with your preferred oil for a more straightforward application.

A light oil coating on both sides of the food can make all the difference.

Another tip is to avoid overcrowding the basket, as this can cause food to stick together or stick to the basket.

Instead, cook smaller batches and shake or toss halfway through cooking for even crisping.

And remember not to use wet batter foods in your air fryer, as these tend to stick and become messy.

How Do I Season My Canned Foods Before Cooking?
Seasoning your canned foods before cooking them in the air fryer is a great way to add flavor and enhance the taste.

You can use different seasonings and spices depending on your preference or recipe.

One easy way to season vegetables, such as green beans, is to sprinkle garlic powder, onion powder, salt, and black pepper.

Advertisements

If you're cooking meats like chicken or fish from cans, adding a dry rub made with chili powder, paprika, cumin, and coriander can give it a smoky and spicy flavor.

You can also mix breadcrumbs with Parmesan cheese for a cheesy coating on baked goods like biscuits or breadsticks.

Experimenting with different seasoning combinations will help you find what works best for your taste buds!

How do I clean the Air Fryer
Again, it depends on the model really, however, the general rule seems to be to soak the basket, and removable bucket in warm soapy water for around 10 minutes before trying to clean it. You can also place the parts into a dishwasher.

Tips For Success In Air Frying Canned Foods
Use tongs or a spatula to flip canned foods halfway through cooking, avoid overcrowding the air fryer basket, shake the basket occasionally, and prepare smaller batches for maximum crispiness.

Using Tongs Or A Spatula To Flip The Food
When air frying canned foods, it's essential to flip them halfway through the cooking process. This ensures even cooking and avoids burnt or undercooked spots.

I recommend using tongs or a spatula to gently flip the food in the basket.

One helpful tip is to spray the food with oil before flipping it over. This helps keep the coating on and prevents sticking.

Using tongs or a spatula also allows you to check if any excess liquid has accumulated in the bottom of the basket and can be drained off for crispier results.

Remember, giving your canned foods a little mid-cook flip will make all the difference in achieving that crispy texture we love from air frying!

Avoiding Overcrowding Of The Air Fryer Basket
One of the critical things to remember when air frying canned foods is to avoid overcrowding the basket. This can lead to uneven cooking and result in some portions being overcooked while others remain undercooked.

To ensure even cooking, it's best to cook smaller batches instead of filling the entire basket.

Another critical tip when avoiding overcrowding is to use tongs or a spatula to flip the food halfway through cooking. This allows both sides of your canned food to be exposed evenly to hot air, resulting in perfectly crispy and delicious results.

Remember that proper spacing between each piece will also help keep your air fryer clean and free from burnt debris.

By following these simple tips for avoiding overcrowding, you'll achieve perfect results whenever you cook canned foods in your air fryer – vegetables, meats, or baked goods!

Shaking The Basket Halfway Through Cooking
Shaking the basket halfway through cooking is essential for air frying canned foods. This helps ensure that all sides of the food are cooked evenly and crisped to perfection.

I usually set a timer halfway through the cooking time to remind me when to give the basket a good shake.

Not shaking the basket can result in unevenly cooked food, with some parts being overcooked while others remain undercooked. This is especially important when air frying has frozen canned foods like vegetables or meats, as they clump together during cooking.

Shaking the basket halfway through ensures all pieces get coated in hot air and cook evenly across all sides.

Preparing Smaller Batches
Preparing smaller batches of canned foods is crucial to achieving the best results in air frying. Overcrowding the air fryer basket can cause uneven cooking and soggy food.

It's important to leave enough space between each piece and flip them halfway through for even browning.

To save time, you can prepare multiple small batches of different foods in advance and cook them separately in your air fryer.

This will also allow you to experiment with different recipes and seasonings without worrying about ruining an entire batch if it doesn't turn out as expected.

Remember that while air frying is a healthier alternative to deep frying, practicing portion control is still essential. Preparing smaller batches ensures better cooking and helps manage serving sizes for a more balanced meal.

POULTRY RECIPES

Chicken Taco Poblano Rice Bowls

Servings: 4   **Cooking Time:** 15 Mins.

Ingredients:
- 1 1/4 pounds organic boneless skinless chicken breasts, cut 1/2 inch cubes (from 3 small)
- 2 teaspoons olive oil
- 1 medium red onion (peeled and diced)
- 1/4 cup cilantro (minced plus more for garnish)
- 1 poblano pepper (seeded and diced)
- 1 roma tomato (cored and diced)
- 1 lime (halved)
- taco seasoning (see below)
- kosher salt
- 1 cup frozen or fresh corn kernels
- 3 cups cooked brown rice (heated (use cauliflower rice for low-carb))
- 1/4 cup cheddar-jack cheese
- 1/4 cup 2% sour cream or Greek yogurt (optional)
- Taco seasoning:
- 1 teaspoon garlic powder
- 1 teaspoon cumin
- 1 teaspoon kosher salt
- 1/2 teaspoon chili powder
- 1/2 teaspoon paprika
- 1/2 teaspoon oregano

Directions:
1. Dice the chicken into small pieces. Combine taco seasoning in a small bowl and set aside.
2. To make the pico de gallo, set 3 tablespoons of the diced onion aside and place it in a bowl with tomato, cilantro, 2 teaspoons lime juice, 1/4 teaspoon salt. Set aside.
3. Add oil to a large skillet over medium-high heat. When hot, add the chicken and cook until it starts to brown, 2 to 3 minutes.
4. Add the remaining onion, poblano pepper and taco seasoning to the skillet and cook until it softens, 2 to 3 minutes. Add 1/2 cup water and corn. Cook 1 to 2 minutes then remove from heat.
5. Divide rice in 4 bowls, top with chicken, cheese, pico de gallo and optional sour cream.

Leftover Turkey Pot Pie Empanadas

Servings: 10   Cooking Time: 30 Mins.

Ingredients:

- 1 teaspoon unsalted butter
- 1/4 cup chopped onion
- 1/4 cup chopped celery
- 2 tablespoons chopped fresh parsley
- 1 clove garlic (minced)
- 1 tablespoon corn starch
- 1/2 cup low sodium chicken or turkey broth
- 1 1/4 cups leftover shredded cooked turkey breast (5 ounces)
- 3/4 cup frozen peas and carrots
- 3/4 teaspoon kosher salt
- 1/8 tsp ground black pepper
- 1/2 tsp dried thyme
- 10 frozen Goya Empanada Discos (the ones for baking, thawed)
- cooking spray
- 1 large egg (whisked)

Directions:

1. Heat a skillet over medium heat, melt butter. Add onion, celery, and parsley cooking until onions are translucent. Add minced garlic, cooking for an additional minute.
2. Combine the broth and cornstarch together and mix well.
3. Add the turkey, frozen peas and carrots, 3/4 teaspoon salt, pepper, thyme and broth, stir and cook medium heat, bring to a boil then cook until thickened and heated through, 2-3 minutes.
4. Place a disc on your work surface. Take 2 tablespoon of the turkey mixture and place in the middle of each disc. Using a pastry brush, place the egg wash on the outer edges of the disc. Fold the disc over and gently press the edges to create a seal. Use a fork and press around the edges to seal.
5. Brush the egg wash over one side of each of the empanadas.
6. Spray the baking sheet with oil, bake 350F 26 to 30 minutes, until golden.
7. Air Fryer:
8. Spray the basket with oil to prevent sticking, transfer to the basket, in batches and cook at 380F° for 8 minutes, turning half way. Eat hot.

Air Fryer Taquitos

Servings: 8   **Cooking Time:** 20 Mins.

Ingredients:

- 2 cups cooked chicken or pork or beef, shredded
- 1 tablespoon taco seasoning
- 4 ounces cream cheese
- 1 tablespoon jalapenos finely diced
- 1 green onion sliced, green and whites divided
- 1 cup Tex Mex cheese shredded
- 8 corn tortillas 6 inches each
- cooking spray

Directions:

1. Combine chicken, taco seasoning and 3 tablespoons water. Simmer 5 minutes or until water is evaporated.
2. Add cream cheese, jalapenos, and the whites of the green onion. Cook until melted and creamy.
3. Place tortillas on a plate, top with a damp paper towel and microwave 40 seconds or until warm.
4. Divide filling over tortillas and top with 2 tablespoons cheese. Roll tightly and secure with a toothpick.
5. Preheat air fryer to 400°F.
6. Spray taquitos with cooking spray or brush with oil. Place in a single layer and cook about 6-8 minutes or until crisp.
7. Cool 2 minutes before serving. Garnish with remaining green onions and toppings as desired.

Air Fryer Roast Chicken

Servings: 2-3

Ingredients:

- Deselect All
- 1 small chicken (3 to 3 1/2 pounds)
- 1 tablespoon olive oil
- Kosher salt and freshly ground black pepper
- 3 sprigs fresh rosemary, thyme, sage or a combination
- 1 head garlic, cut in half to expose all the cloves
- 1/2 lemon

Directions:

1. Preheat a 3.5-quart air fryer to 370 degrees F.
2. Rub the outside of the chicken with the olive oil, then sprinkle the chicken inside and out with 1 tablespoon salt and several grinds of pepper. Fill the cavity with the herbs, garlic and lemon. Put the chicken in the air fryer basket breast-side up, pushing it down so it does not touch the top of the fryer.
3. Roast the chicken until it is golden and crispy and an instant-read thermometer inserted in the thickest part of the thigh, avoiding bone, reads 165 degrees F, 50 to 60 minutes.

Air Fryer Bbq Chicken Drumsticks

Servings: 4

Ingredients:

- 8 chicken drumsticks (about 2 lb.)
- 1/2 tsp. kosher salt
- 1/4 tsp. freshly ground black pepper
- 3 tsp. extra-virgin olive oil
- 1 large clove garlic, minced
- 3/4 c. ketchup
- 1/2 c. cider vinegar
- 2 tbsp. dark brown sugar
- 2 tsp. smoked paprika
- 1/2 tsp. ground cumin
- Chopped fresh parsley leaves, for garnish

Directions:

1. In a large bowl, toss chicken, salt, pepper, and 2 teaspoons oil. Working in batches if necessary, in an air-fryer basket, arrange drumsticks, spacing about 1/2" apart. Cook at 400° for 10 minutes.
2. Meanwhile, in a small saucepan over medium-high heat, cook garlic and remaining 1 teaspoon oil, stirring, until golden and fragrant, about 1 minute. Add ketchup, vinegar, brown sugar, paprika, and cumin. Bring to a boil. Reduce heat to medium and simmer until sauce coats back of a spoon, about 10 minutes (you should have about 1 cup sauce). Transfer half of sauce to a large heatproof bowl; reserve remaining sauce for serving.
3. Toss chicken with sauce in large bowl. Return chicken to air fryer, discarding any excess sauce left in bowl, and continue to cook at 400° until chicken is cooked through and charred in spots, 7 to 10 minutes more.
4. Arrange chicken on a platter. Top with parsley. Serve with reserved sauce alongside.

Air Fryer Turkey Legs

 Servings: 3   Cooking Time: 30 Mins.

Ingredients:

- 3 turkey legs
- 4 tablespoons butter, melted
- 1 teaspoon Cajun seasoning
- ½ teaspoon poultry seasoning
- ¼ teaspoon garlic salt
- ¼ teaspoon pepper
- ¼ teaspoon paprika

Directions:

1. Preheat your air fryer to 390 degrees F.
2. Add the melted butter, cajun and poultry seasoning, garlic salt, pepper, and paprika in a bowl and mix.
3. Baste the seasoned butter all over the turkey legs top and bottom and sides.
4. Place the turkey legs in the air fryer basket and cook for 25-30 minutes until they reach an internal temperature of 165 degrees F.
5. Remove the turkey legs from the air fryer and enjoy!

Notes:

1. HOW TO REHEAT TURKEY LEGS IN THE AIR FRYER:
2. Preheat the air fryer to 350 degrees F.
3. Place the turkey legs in a single layer in the air fryer basket.
4. Cook for about 5 minutes until heated through.

Air-fryer Chicken Wings With Buffalo Sauce

 Servings: 6   Cooking Time: 30 Mins.

Ingredients:

- 1kg Macro free-range chicken wing nibbles
- 2 tsp baking powder
- 50g butter
- 1/4 cup hot sauce
- 1 tsp Worcestershire sauce
- 1 tsp brown sugar
- 2/3 cup yoghurt ranch dressing
- 1 stalk celery, cut into sticks
- 4 radishes, halved
- 4 Qukes® baby cucumbers, halved
- 125g snow peas, blanched, halved

Directions:

1. Preheat air fryer to 180°C for 3 minutes. Place chicken in a large bowl. Sprinkle over baking powder, then toss to coat. Place chicken in basket. Slide pan and basket into appliance. Set timer for 30 minutes. Cook, turning occasionally, or until golden and cooked through.
2. During the last 5 minutes of cooking, melt butter in a small frying pan over medium heat. Add sauces and sugar, then bring to the boil. Remove pan from heat.
3. Transfer Chicken To A Large Bowl, Then Add Hot-Sauce Mixture And Toss To Coat. Serve Wings With Ranch Dressing, Celery, Radish, Cucumber And Snow Peas.

Air Fryer Chicken Thighs

Servings: 4 **Cooking Time:** 12 Mins.

Ingredients:
- 4 large bone-in chicken thighs
- 2 tablespoons olive oil
- 1/2 teaspoon smoked paprika
- 1/2 teaspoon Italian seasonings
- 1/2 teaspoon garlic powder
- 1/2 teaspoon pepper
- 1/2 teaspoon salt

Directions:
1. Preheat the air fryer to 190C/375F.
2. In a bowl, add the chicken and oil and mix together. Add the salt, pepper, and spices and mix well.
3. Place chicken, skin side up, in an air fryer basket. Cook for 13-17 minutes, or until the chicken reaches an internal temperature of 165F. Be sure to flip halfway through.
4. Remove the chicken thighs from the air fryer and let them sit for five minutes before serving.

Notes:
1. TO STORE: Leftovers can be stored in an air tight container for up to five days.
2. TO FREEZE: Place the cooked and cooled chicken in a ziplock bag and store it in the freezer for up to three months.
3. TO REHEAT: Thaw the frozen air fryer chicken thighs overnight before reheating in the air fryer, oven, or even microwave.

Bbq Chicken Wings Cooking In Air Fryer

Servings: 3-4 **Cooking Time:** 25 Mins.

Ingredients:
- 1 ½ lbs of chicken wings, wings and flats separated, tips discarded
- 2 teaspoons Stubbs BBQ rub
- ¼ - ½ cup BBQ sauce

Directions:
1. Preheat your air fryer to 380 degrees F. Pat the chicken wings dry and coat them evenly with the BBQ rub.
2. Place the wings in the air fryer basket in a single layer, leaving room between the wings.
3. Cook for 20 minutes, flipping the wings halfway through.
4. Turn the temperature to 400 degrees and cook for another 3 to 5 minutes.
5. Remove the wings from the air fryer and toss them in the BBQ sauce. Return to your air fryer for another 1 to 2 minutes to heat up the sauce, or serve right away.
6. Remove the BBQ chicken wings from the air fryer and enjoy!

Air Fryer Chicken Breast

Servings: 2 **Cooking Time:** 8 Mins.

Ingredients:

- 2 boneless, skinless chicken breasts
- 1/2 teaspoon kosher salt
- 2 teaspoons olive oil
- 1 teaspoon paprika
- ½ teaspoon garlic powder
- ½ teaspoon onion powder
- ¼ teaspoon black pepper

Directions:

1. Place the chicken breasts on a cutting board and cover with a large sheet of plastic wrap. With a rolling pin, meat mallet, or your palm, lightly pound into an even thickness.
2. To Dry Brine*: Place the chicken on a plate and sprinkle all over with the kosher salt. Place in the refrigerator uncovered for at least 30 minutes or up to 1 day—if you will not be dry brining, skip this step.
3. When ready to air fry: remove the chicken from the refrigerator and let stand at room temperature for 15 minutes.
4. In a small bowl, stir together the paprika, garlic powder, onion powder, and black pepper (if you did not dry brine the chicken, add the salt now)
5. Place the chicken in a large bowl and drizzle with the olive oil. Sprinkle the spice mixture over the top. Toss to coat the chicken, ensuring you rub the spices evenly over both sides.
6. Preheat the air fryer to 375 degrees F (my model takes 3 minutes to heat). Place the chicken presentation side (smooth side) down in the air fryer and let cook 6 minutes.
7. Remove the air fryer basket, then with tongs, carefully flip the chicken over. Continue cooking until the chicken registers between 155 and 160 degrees F, 2 to 8 minutes more. Chicken is considered safe to eat at 165 degrees F, but I like to remove mine a few degrees early, then let the carryover cooking finish the job. The total cook time will vary based on your model and the size of your chicken. Smaller breasts (about 6 ounces each) will need only around 8 minutes total; larger ones may need 14 or more. Check the chicken often towards the end to monitor its progress. DO NOT overcook or it will be dry.
8. Remove the chicken to a plate. Cover and let rest 5 to 10 minutes. Slice and enjoy!

Notes:

1. *While dry brining isn't 100% mandatory (the spices, cooking temperature, and cook times listed in this recipe are still correct for the best air fryer chicken breasts), brining works magic on meat. It improves its texture (it makes it juicy, plump, and meaty, not rubbery) and its flavor, because the meat will taste more seasoned all the way through, not just on the outside. If you have time for brining, I highly recommend it.
2. This is the air fryer I used for testing. Total cook time may vary based on your model.
3. No air fryer? Make my juicy Baked Chicken Breast instead.
4. TO STORE: Refrigerate chicken breasts in an airtight storage container for up to 4 days.
5. TO REHEAT: Gently rewarm chicken in the air fryer or oven at 350 degrees F.
6. TO FREEZE: Freeze leftovers in an airtight freezer-safe storage container for up to 3 months. Let thaw overnight in the refrigerator before reheating.

Air Fryer Chicken Milanese With Arugula

Servings: 4　　**Cooking Time:** 15 Mins.

Ingredients:
- 2 boneless, skinless chicken breasts (16 oz total)
- 3/4 teaspoon kosher salt
- Freshly ground black pepper
- 1/2 cup seasoned whole wheat breadcrumbs (wheat or gluten-free)
- 2 tablespoons grated Parmesan cheese
- 1 large egg (beaten)
- olive oil spray
- 6 cups baby arugula
- 3 lemons (cut into wedges)

Directions:
1. Cut chicken into 4 cutlets, then place cutlets between 2 sheets of parchment paper or plastic wrap and pound out to 1/4-inch thick.
2. Sprinkle both sides with salt and pepper.
3. In a shallow plate, beat the egg and 1 teaspoon of water together.
4. Combine breadcrumbs and parmesan cheese in a shallow bowl.
5. Dip the chicken into the egg, then the breadcrumb mixture. Place on a work surface and spray both sides with olive oil.
6. Preheat the air fryer to 400F.
7. In batches transfer to the air fryer basket and cook 7 minutes, turning halfway until golden and cooked through.
8. Serve chicken with 1 1/2 cups arugula and top with a generous amount of lemon juice.
9. Oven Directions:
10. Bake in a preheated oven 425F 425F for 12 to 14 minutes, flipping halfway until golden.

Air Fryer Frozen Chicken Nuggets

Servings: 2　　**Cooking Time:** 9 Mins.

Ingredients:
- 16 chicken nuggets frozen
- bbq sauce or honey mustard for dipping

Directions:
1. Preheat air fryer to 400°F.
2. Place chicken nuggets in a single layer in the air fryer basket.
3. Cook for 8-9 minutes or until golden and crispy.

Air Fryer Asian Whole Roasted Chicken

Servings: 4-6   **Cooking Time:** 60 Mins.

Ingredients:
- 1 tablespoon brown sugar
- 3 tablespoons oyster sauce
- 1 tablespoon sesame oil
- 1 cup soy sauce
- 1 tablespoon cornstarch
- ¼ teaspoon black pepper
- ¼ teaspoon crushed red pepper flakes
- 1 whole chicken (3 to 4 pounds), washed and patted dry
- oil, for spraying

Directions:
1. In a small bowl, combine brown sugar, oyster sauce, sesame oil, soy sauce, cornstarch, black pepper, and red pepper flakes. Pour mixture into large ziplock bag. Add chicken and marinade for 24 hours. Turn occasionally.
2. Pat chicken dry, spray with oil, and place in air fryer basket, breast-side down. Set temperature to 350°F, and cook for 30 minutes. Turn chicken, spray with oil, and cook for 30 minutes more, or until internal temperature on a meat thermometer reaches 165 degrees in the thickest part of the thigh. Carve and serve warm.
3. Cook's Note: For maximum flavor, marinade he chicken a day before you plan to cook it.

Simple Chicken Breasts

Servings: 3   **Cooking Time:** 26 Mins.

Ingredients:
- 3 (2-inch thick) boneless, skinless chicken breasts
- 1 teaspoon kosher salt
- 1 teaspoon freshly ground black pepper
- Olive oil spray

Directions:
1. Select the Preheat function on the Air Fryer, adjust the temperature to 390°F, then press Start/Pause.
2. Spray both sides of the chicken breasts with oil spray and season with kosher salt and black pepper.
3. Place the chicken breasts into the preheated air fryer basket.
4. Set the temperature to 390°F and time to 26 minutes, then press Start/Pause.
5. Flip the chicken breasts halfway through the cooking time.
6. Remove the chicken when done, let rest for 5 minutes then serve.

Air Fryer Chimichangas

Servings: 8 **Cooking Time:** 17 Mins.

Ingredients:
- For the Chicken:
- 4 cups of deli-style cooked shredded rotisserie chicken or shredded chicken breast
- 1 large onion, finely chopped
- 1 4oz. can chopped green chilies
- 4 tbsp all-purpose flour
- 1 16 oz can of red enchilada sauce.
- ¼ tsp garlic powder
- 1 tsp ground cumin
- 8 (6 in) flour tortillas
- Toppings for Chimichangas (optional)
- Reduced Fat Cheddar Cheese
- Plain Greek Yogurt
- Cilantro or Scallions

Directions:
1. Preheat air fryer to 400°F. Coat a large skillet with cooking spray.
2. Add onions and green chilies to pan and saute for 2 minutes. When the onions are soft add flour, salt, cumin, garlic powder, enchilada sauce, and continue stirring. When the sauce has thickened add in precooked shredded chicken. If the sauce looks too thick add in some chicken stock to thin it out. (2 tablespoons to start)
3. Take off heat and begin preparing the chimichangas for cooking them in the air fryer.
4. Assemble chimichangas by spooning about 1/2 cup of chicken mixture onto each tortilla; fold in sides and roll up.
5. Spray the outside of each filled tortilla with cooking spray; place 4 in the basket of air fryer, seam side down. Set to 400°F; cook 4 minutes. Turn; cook 2 to 3 minutes or until lightly browned and heated through. Repeat with remaining 4 filled tortillas.

FISH & SEAFOOD RECIPES

Air Fryer Fish Tacos

Servings: 8 **Cooking Time: 10 Mins.**

Ingredients:

- For the Tacos:
- 1 lb white fish halibut or cod is best
- 1 tsp chili powder
- 1/2 tsp oregano
- 1/2 tsp garlic powder
- 1 tsp paprika
- 1/4 tsp cayenne
- 1/4 tsp cumin
- 1/2 tsp salt
- 1/4 tsp black pepper
- 1 egg beaten
- 1/2 cup flour
- 1 cup breadcrumbs I use panko
- cooking spray
- 8 corn tortillas
- For the Coleslaw
- 1/2 cup sour cream
- 1/4 cup mayonnaise
- 1/4 cup fresh cilantro chopped
- 2 cloves garlic minced
- 1 tbsp lime juice
- salt to taste
- 1 cup cole slaw mix
- Garnish:
- sliced avocado

Directions:

1. Prepare the slaw by adding all of the slaw ingredients into a medium mixing bowl and mix to combine thoroughly. Set aside.
2. In a small mixing bowl, add the chili powder, oregano, garlic powder, paprika, cayenne, cumin and salt and pepper. Add the seasoning to the fish and cut into 1.5" length pieces.
3. Prepare the dredging stations- in a shallow plate add the flour, in another add the eggs, and in the final add the breadcrumbs.
4. One at a time, dip each fish piece into the flour, then the egg, and finally the breadcrumbs. Press the breadcrumbs into the fish to help it stick.
5. Add the fish pieces into the air fryer basket on a single layer and cook at 390 F for 8 to 10 minutes, until each piece has turned golden.
6. Assemble the tacos by placing some cooked fish into each tortilla and then spoon the slaw on top. Garnish with sliced avocado if desired. Serve immediately.

Notes:

1. The thickness of the fish will determine the cooking time. If you're unsure if your fish is cooked through, use an instant-read thermometer ?. The fish should have an internal temperature of 145F.
2. Make sure you do not overlap the fish pieces in the air fryer. The hot air needs to circulate and reach every part of the fish to crisp up.
3. You can warm up the tortillas before assembling the tacos, so they are more pliable. You can warm them in a skillet or on a stovetop burner.
4. If there is moisture on the fish, pat dry before coating with seasoning to help it stick better.

Crispy Air Fryer Shrimp

Servings: 4   **Cooking Time:** 20 Mins.

Ingredients:
- ¼ cup flour
- 1 ½ teaspoons lemon pepper seasoning
- ½ teaspoon garlic powder
- ½ teaspoon salt or to taste
- ⅓ cup seasoned bread crumbs
- ⅓ cup Panko bread crumbs
- 2 large eggs beaten
- ¾ pound large shrimp with tails peeled and deveined
- cooking spray

Directions:
1. Combine flour and half of the seasonings. In a separate bowl, combine bread crumbs and remaining seasonings.
2. Preheat air fryer to 400°F for 5 minutes.
3. Toss shrimp in the flour mixture. Remove a shrimp from the flour mixture and dip in egg and then into the breadcrumb mixture. Repeat with remaining shrimp.
4. Lightly spray shrimp with cooking spray.
5. Add a single layer of shrimp to the air fryer basket. Cook 4 minutes.
6. Flip shrimp over, spritz with cooking spray and cook an additional 4 minutes or just until cooked through and crispy.
7. Repeat with remaining shrimp.
8. Serve with cocktail sauce.

Notes:
1. Smaller shrimp may need a minute or so less cook time.
2. Leftovers will last up to 3 days in an airtight container in the fridge.
3. To reheat, place on a baking sheet in a 350°F oven for up to 10 minutes or until crispy.

Air Fryer Fish Cakes

Servings: 4   **Cooking Time:** 10 Mins.

Ingredients:

- 12 ounces cod fillets, or any other white fish, coarsely chopped
- ⅔ cup pork rind panko crumbs, you can also use regular breadcrumbs
- 2 tablespoons finely chopped fresh cilantro
- 2 tablespoons sweet chili sauce
- 2 tablespoons mayonnaise
- 1 egg
- ¼ teaspoon salt, or to taste
- ¼ teaspoon fresh ground black pepper, or to taste
- Lime wedges, for serving

Directions:

1. Preheat air fryer to 400°F.
2. Grease the basket of the air fryer with non-aerosol cooking spray, or line it with parchment paper.
3. Transfer the chopped fish to a food processor and process until crumbly. (see notes below)
4. In a bowl combine the crumbled fish, pork rind crumbs, cilantro, chili sauce, mayo, egg, salt, and pepper; stir until well incorporated.
5. Shape the mixture into four patties.
6. Place the patties in the air fryer basket and coat them with cooking spray.
7. Cook for 5 minutes; flip over the fish cakes, spray with cooking spray, and continue to cook for 4 to 5 more minutes, or until golden brown and crispy.
8. Remove from air fryer basket.
9. Serve fish cakes with lime wedges.

Notes:

1. If you don't have a food processor, chop the fish until finely minced.
2. NET CARBS: 3g

Air Fryer Salmon Cakes

Servings: 4   **Cooking Time:** 10 Mins.

Ingredients:

- 14.75 oz salmon canned, deboned
- 2 eggs
- 1 tbsp mayonnaise
- 1/2 bell pepper red
- 1/2 cup breadcrumbs
- 1/2 tsp garlic powder
- 1/2 tsp black pepper
- 1/4 tsp salt
- 2 tbsp fresh chopped parsley
- 1 tsp olive oil spray

Directions:

1. Heat the air fryer to 390 degrees Fahrenheit. Prepare the Air Fryer basket.
2. Mix the salmon, breadcrumbs, eggs, and seasonings in a large bowl.
3. Measure out the salmon patties with ½ cup measuring cup.
4. Form the salmon cakes to be no larger than 1" thickness.
5. Add the salmon cakes to the prepared air fryer basket. Spray the tops of the patties and cook for 8 minutes.
6. Open the Air Fryer and flip the patties over, spray the top of the patties, and cook for an additional 2 minutes.
7. Serve with dill sauce or favorite dipping sauce.

Notes:

1. DO I NEED TO REMOVE THE BONES FROM CANNED SALMON BEFORE USING?
2. Yes, unless you want to eat the bones (at your own risk!) for the extra calcium. The canning process does make the salmon bones softer and easily mashed and edible. I personally prefer to remove them.
3. HOW DO I STORE LEFTOVER SALMON CAKES?
4. Store leftover salmon cakes in an airtight container in the refrigerator for up to 3 days.
5. HOW DO I REHEAT LEFTOVER SALMON CAKES?
6. To reheat refrigerated salmon cakes, place them in the preheated air fryer and cook at 350 degrees Fahrenheit for 3-5 minutes, or until heated thoroughly.

Air Fryer Fish & Chips

Servings: 4   **Cooking Time:** 30 Mins.

Ingredients:
- Chips
- 2 baking potatoes scrubbed and cut into ¼" fries
- 2 tablespoons olive oil
- ½ teaspoon seasoned salt
- Fish
- 1 cup flour
- ½ cup buttermilk
- 1 egg
- 1 cup panko bread crumbs
- 2 teaspoons lemon pepper
- 1 pound cod fillets or other white fish

Directions:
1. Chips
2. Soak fries in cold water for 30 minutes.
3. Drain fries and dab dry with paper towels. Toss with oil and salt.
4. Preheat air fryer to 390°F.
5. Place the potatoes in the basket and cook for 17 minutes or until crisp. Shake the basket after 10 minutes. Remove from the air fryer and set aside.
6. Fish
7. While fries are cooking, place flour in a shallow dish and season with salt and pepper to taste.
8. In a separate bowl, whisk buttermilk and egg. In a third bowl, combine Panko and lemon pepper.
9. Dry fish and dip into the egg mixture and then into flour mixture.
10. Dip back into the egg mixture and then into the Panko mixture. Spray generously with cooking spray.
11. Add fish to the empty air fryer basket and cook at 390°F for 11-13 minutes or until cooked through and flaky. Do not overcook.
12. Add fries to the air fryer basket and cook until heated through, about 2 minutes.

Notes:
1. Thicker fish may need longer, and thinner fish filets may cook faster.
2. Appliances can vary by appliance. Check both fish and the fries frequently to ensure they don't overcook.
3. Frozen fries can be used and will only take about 7-9 minutes to cook.

Air Fryer Low Country Boil

Servings: 2   **Cooking Time:** 10 Mins.

Ingredients:
- 1 cup dry white wine (or water)
- 2 ears corn, cut in half
- ½ pound shrimp
- 6 littleneck clams
- 1 pound andouille sausage, cut into 1-inch pieces
- 2 lobster tails (4 ounces each)
- 1 lemon, cut in half
- 1 tablespoon shrimp boil seasoning

Directions:
1. Place wine in bottom pan of air fryer, set temperature to 400 degrees, and preheat for 5 minutes.
2. Add air fryer basket to air fryer pan, leaving wine in place, and fill basket with corn, shrimp, clams, andouille sausage, and lobster tails. Squeeze lemon halves over top of seafood mixture, sprinkle with shrimp boil seasoning, and place lemon halves on top of lobster tails. Set temperature to 350 degrees, and steam for 10 minutes. Serve warm.

Air Fryer Scallops With Lemon Cream Sauce

Ingredients:
- 1 pound scallops
- 1 tablespoon olive oil
- 2 cloves garlic, minced
- 1/4 teaspoon red pepper flakes
- 1/2 cup chicken broth
- 1/2 cup heavy cream
- 3 tablespoons lemon juice
- 1/2 teaspoon dried basil
- Kosher salt and freshly ground black pepper, to taste

Directions:
1. Prepare your air fryer basket by spraying it with cooking oil.
2. Add scallops to air fryer basket in a single layer.
3. Air fry at 400°F for 8-10 minutes, flipping halfway through.
4. While scallops are in the air fryer, prepare the lemon cream sauce.
5. Add olive oil, garlic, and red pepper flakes to a skillet.
6. Cook, stirring frequently, until fragrant. This should take about 1-2 minutes.
7. Stir in chicken broth, heavy cream, lemon juice and basil. Season with salt and pepper, to taste.
8. Bring to a boil. Reduce heat and simmer until slightly thickened. This will take about 3-5 minutes.
9. Drizzle over air fried scallops.

Seafood Boil In The Steam Air Fryer

Ingredients:

- 16 oz. extra large shrimp, peeled and deveined
- 12 oz. scallops
- 12 oz. andouille sausage
- 4 sweet corn on the cob
- 1 jumbo red onion
- 1 1/2 lb. petite red potatoes
- 1.5 sticks butter, melted
- 8 cloves garlic, minced
- 1 Tbsp. cajun seasoning
- 1 Tbsp. lemon pepper seasoning
- 1 Tbsp. Old Bay seasoning
- 1 Tbsp. cayenne pepper

Directions:

1. First, remove the water tank from the top of the Steam Air Fryer, fill it with water and return it to the top of the air fryer.
2. Next, remove the crisper tray from the air fryer basket.
3. Add in the red potatoes and the corn. Steam at 212F for about 25 minutes, or until the potatoes are almost cooked through. You can save time on this step if you cut your potatoes in half!
4. Melt the butter in a bowl and mix in the garlic and all the seasonings. Reserve 1/2 of the butter mixture and set aside.
5. Once the potatoes and corn are done cooking, add the onion, sausage, scallops and shrimp into the basket.
6. Add in 1/2 of the butter mixture and toss everything to coat.
7. Steam again at 212F for 15 minutes, or until the seafood is fully cooked.
8. Once finished, dump the basket on a large platter or sheet pan. Drizzle the remaining butter mixture all over and enjoy!

Easy Air Fryer Lemon Garlic Salmon Recipe

Servings: 4   Cooking Time: 11 Mins.

Ingredients:

- 4 6 oz salmon filets
- 2 tbsp olive oil
- 2 tsp garlic powder
- 1 tsp celtic sea salt
- 1 tsp fresh cracked pepper
- 1 lemon, sliced into thin rounds
- 1 tsp lemon juice (I put a flexible cutting board down when slicing my lemon, as I'll usually just use the juice that comes from cutting it.)
- 2 tsp Italian herbs

Directions:

1. In a large bowl, drizzle lemon juice and olive oil over salmon and rub to make sure the salmon filets are evenly coated.
2. Season generously with salt, pepper, and Italian herbs.
3. Arrange salmon filets in air fryer basket, making sure they dont touch too much (don"t over crowd the basket, so air can move around salmon easily).
4. Arrange lemon slices on and around salmon in air fryer basket.
5. Set air fryer to 400 degrees and cook for 10 minutes for salmon with a little bit of red in the middle.
6. Cook for 12 minutes for salmon with no red in the middle, 14 for well done salmon or thicker salmon filets.
7. Serve and enjoy!

Air Fryer Miso-ginger Salmon Recipe

Servings: 2   **Cooking Time:** 15-20 Mins.

Ingredients:
- 1 (1-inch) piece fresh ginger
- 1 clove garlic
- 2 tablespoons white miso paste
- 1 tablespoon soy sauce or tamari
- 1 tablespoon maple syrup or honey
- 2 teaspoons toasted sesame oil
- 1/4 plus 1/8 teaspoon kosher salt, divided
- Freshly ground black pepper
- 2 (6-ounce) salmon filets
- 1 medium bunch broccolini (about 6 ounces)
- 2 teaspoons olive oil

Directions:
1. Prepare the following, adding each to a shallow container that fits the salmon in a single layer (such as a pie plate or loaf pan) as you complete it: Peel and finely grate a 1-inch piece of ginger (about 1 teaspoon). Finely grate 1 garlic clove.
2. Add 2 tablespoons white miso paste, 1 tablespoon soy sauce or tamari, 2 teaspoons maple syrup or honey, 2 teaspoons sesame oil, 1/4 teaspoon of the kosher salt, and a few grinds black pepper. Whisk until mostly smooth, some small lumps are ok.
3. Pat 2 (6-ounce) salmon fillets dry with paper towels. Place in the marinade and rub the marinade all over until evenly coated. Arrange skin side up. Cover and let marinate in the refrigerator for 1 hour.
4. Remove from the refrigerator and let sit at room temperature while you prepare the broccolini.
5. Heat an air fryer to 375°F. Meanwhile, trim 1 medium bunch broccolini. Place in a bowl or plate. Drizzle with 2 teaspoons olive oil and season with the remaining 1/8 teaspoon kosher salt and a few grinds black pepper. Toss to coat.
6. Place the broccolini in the air fryer basket or tray in a single layer. Air fry until crisp-tender and the edges are lightly browned, 7 to 8 minutes. Transfer to a plate and loosely cover with aluminum foil to keep warm while you air fry the salmon.
7. Heat the air fryer to 400°F. Coat the air fryer basket or tray with cooking spray.
8. Remove the salmon from the marinade and place skin-side down in the basket or tray. Discard any remaining marinade. Air fry until golden-brown on top and the flesh flakes at the end of the fillet when gently tested with a fork, 8 to 12 minutes. Serve with the broccolini

Notes:
1. Storage: Refrigerate leftovers in an airtight container for up to 2 days.

Air Fryer Lemon & Garlic Tuna Steak

Servings: 4   **Cooking Time:** 10 Mins.

Ingredients:

- 600g tuna steaks
- 2 tbs olive oil
- 1 large lemon, juice and zest
- 2 cloves garlic, peeled and minced
- 1 tsp oregano, dried
- 200g kale
- 200g tenderstem broccoli

Directions:

1. Whisk the olive oil, lemon juice and zest and garlic together in a small bowl. Place the tuna steaks in a baking dish and brush each with the oil, reserving 1 teaspoon. Cover and leave to marinate for 30 minutes.
2. Heat the air fryer to 180°C. Sprinkle the steaks with oregano and place in the air fryer basket. Cook for 8 minutes.
3. Heat the remaining infused oil in a large pan on medium high heat and cook the broccoli for 3 minutes, stir in the kale and cook for 2 more minutes, until wilted, adding a dash of water if necessary.
4. Serve the tuna steaks with the sauteed greens and lemon wedges on the side, if desired.

Air Fryer Salmon With Dill

Servings: 2   **Cooking Time:** 7 Mins.

Ingredients:

- 1 tablespoon olive oil
- 1 teaspoon lemon juice
- 2 salmon filets 5-6 oz each
- ¼ teaspoon dried dill
- ¼ teaspoon lemon pepper seasoning
- salt and pepper to taste

Directions:

1. Preheat air fryer to 400°F.
2. Combine olive oil and lemon juice together and brush over the salmon.
3. Mix the dill and lemon pepper together and evenly coat the filets.
4. Place them in the air fryer basket and cook for 6-7 minutes or until they start to flake. (Reaching 145°F internally)
5. Notes
6. To cook frozen filets add 3-4 minutes to the cooking time, or air fry until the internal temperature reaches 145°F.
7. Leftover salmon filets will keep in the refrigerator for up to 3 days or in the freezer for 1 month.

Air Fryer Scalloped Potatoes

Servings: 6 **Cooking Time: 20 Mins.**

Ingredients:

- 2 tablespoons butter
- ¼ large onion diced
- 1 clove garlic minced
- 2 tablespoons flour
- ½ cups milk or cream
- 1 cup chicken broth
- 2 pounds yellow potatoes about 6 medium potatoes, sliced about ⅛" thick
- ½ teaspoon salt or to taste
- ⅛ teaspoon pepper or to taste

Directions:

1. Preheat the air fryer to 400°F. Grease an 8-inch pan or one that will fit in your air fryer.
2. Potatoes
3. Toss potatoes with olive oil in a large bowl and place in a single layer in the air fryer basket. Cook for 8-10 minutes until softened. This may need to be done in batches, depending on the size of your air fryer. Set aside.
4. Sauce
5. Melt butter, onion, and garlic over medium heat. Cook until onion is softened, about 3 minutes. Add flour and cook for 1-2 minutes.
6. Whisk in chicken broth and milk a little bit at a time until smooth. Continue stirring until the sauce thickens. Let boil 1 minute. Stir in salt and pepper.
7. Assembly
8. Place ⅓ of the potatoes in an even layer in the bottom of the pan. Pour ⅓ of the cream sauce over top.
9. Repeat layers ending with cream sauce. Cover with tin foil and place in the air fryer basket. Reduce the temperature to 375°F and cook for 10 minutes.
10. Uncover and bake for an additional 5-10 minutes or until golden brown and heated through.
11. Allow to rest for 15 minutes before serving.

Air Fryer Beer Battered Fish Tacos

Ingredients:

- Fish:
- 2 cod filets or other white-fleshed fish
- 2 eggs
- 1 1/4 cup lager beer
- 1 1/2 cup all-purpose flour
- 3/4 tsp baking powder
- salt & pepper
- Topping:
- 1/2 c. of corn (fresh or canned)
- 2 tbsp diced red onion
- 1 small tomato (diced)
- 1 cup iceberg lettuce (shredded)
- juice of 1 lime
- 1/4 c. fresh chopped cilantro
- 1 diced jalepeño pepper (optional)
- salt & pepper
- 4 small tortillas

Directions:

1. In a medium-sized bowl, whisk together eggs and beer, then set aside. In a separate medium bowl whisk together flour, baking powder and ¼ teaspoon each of salt and pepper.
2. Slice the fish fillets in half so that you have 4 pieces. Dip fish in batter, then dip into flour mixture, coating all sides.
3. Lightly oil the bottom of the air fryer basket to prevent sticking. Air fry for 10-15 minutes on 400°F.
4. Combine topping ingredients and set aside. Check fish and cook until golden brown. Serve fish and toppings with tortillas.

Air Fryer Cod

Servings: 4 **Cooking Time: 10 Mins.**

Ingredients:

- 4 6-oz Cod fillets
- 1 tbsp Lemon juice (freshly squeezed, from 1/2 a lemon)
- 1 tsp Lemon zest (from 1 lemon)
- 2 tbsp Olive oil
- 1 tsp Sea salt
- 1/2 tsp Black pepper
- 3/4 tsp Paprika
- 1/2 tsp Garlic powder
- 1/8 tsp Cayenne pepper (optional)
- Cooking spray

Directions:

1. Preheat the air fryer to 400 degrees F (204 degrees C).
2. Pat each fish fillet dry with paper towels.
3. In a small bowl, stir together salt, pepper, paprika, garlic powder and cayenne. Set aside.
4. In a separate small bowl, stir together olive oil, lemon juice and lemon zest.
5. Brush each cod fillet with the olive oil/lemon mixture (on both sides). Sprinkle seasoning on both sides and pat gently (so it sticks to the fish).
6. Lightly spray the air fryer basket with cooking spray. Place the cod in the air fryer basket (do not crowd the basket, cook in batches if necessary). Cook for 8-10 minutes, until golden brown on top and 140-145 degrees F (60-63 degrees C) in the center of the largest fillet.

BEEF, PORK & LAMB RECIPES

Air Fryer Lamb Loin Chops With Chimichurri Sauce

Servings: 3 **Cooking Time: 15 Mins.**

Ingredients:

- FOR THE LAMB CHOPS
- 1 lb. lamb chops , each cut about 1-inch thick (@4-5 chops)
- 1/2 teaspoon smoked paprika
- salt , to taste
- black pepper , to taste
- oil spray
- CHIMICHURRI SAUCE
- 1/4 cup olive oil
- 1/3 cup minced fresh parsley
- 1-2 cloves garlic , minced or crushed
- 1/4 teaspoon salt , or to taste
- 1/4 teaspoon black pepper , to taste
- 1-2 pinches red pepper flakes , or to taste
- 1 Tablespoon lemon juice , or to taste

Directions:

1. Make the chimichurri sauce: combine the olive oil, parsley, garlic, salt, black pepper, red pepper flakes, and lemon juice. Taste for seasoning. Set aside.
2. Spray the lamb chops with oil to lightly coat. Season lamb chops with smoked paprika, salt, and black pepper.
3. Spray air fryer basket/tray with oil spray and place lamb chops in a single layer, making sure not to overlap the meat.
4. Air Fry at 380°F/195°C for 8 minutes, flip and continue Air Frying for another 4-8 minutes, or to your preferred doneness. Serve with chimichurri sauce on lamb chops.

Air Fryer Italian Pork Chops Parmigiana

Servings: 3 **Cooking Time:** 18 Mins.

Ingredients:

- 3 (6 oz.) (170g) pork chops, rinsed & patted dry
- salt, to taste
- black pepper, to taste
- garlic powder, to taste
- smoked paprika, to taste
- 1/2 cup (54 g) breadcrumbs, approximately
- 1/2 cup (50 g) grated parmesan cheese
- 2 Tablespoons (30 ml) chopped Italian parsley, plus more for optional garnish
- 1 large egg
- Cooking spray, for coating the pork chops
- 1/2 cup (56 g) grated mozzarella cheese
- 1 cup (240 ml) marinara sauce, heated

Directions:

1. Season the pork chops with salt, pepper, garlic powder, and smoked paprika.
2. Mix together the breadcrumbs, parmesan cheese, and chopped parsley in a bowl. In a separate bowl, beat the egg.
3. Dip each pork chop in egg and then dredge it in the breadcrumb mixture, coating completely. Lightly spray both sides of coated pork chops with cooking spray right before cooking.
4. Preheat the Air Fryer at 380°F for 4 minutes. This will give the breaded pork chops a great sear.
5. Lay pork chops in Air Fryer and cook at 380°F (194°C) for 8-12 minutes. After 6 minutes of cooking, flip the pork chops and then continue cooking for the remainder of time or until golden and internal temperature reaches 145-160°F.
6. Top with cheese and air fry for 2 more minutes to melt the cheese. Serve warm with marinara sauce.

Notes:

1. Recipes were cooked in 3-4 qt air fryers. If using a larger air fryer, the recipe might cook quicker so adjust cooking time.
2. If cooking in multiple batches & not pre-heating before first batch, the first batch will take longer to cook.
3. Remember to set a timer to shake/flip/toss the food as directed in recipe.
4. Preheating the Air Fryer is preferable. If you don't preheat, add more time to the cooking.

Prosciutto Wrapped Figs With Blue Cheese

 Servings: 4   Cooking Time: 5 Mins.

Ingredients:

- Figs:
- 8 large figs
- 1/4 cup blue cheese ((2 ounces) crumbled)
- 4 thin strips prosciutto (cut in half lengthwise (2 ounces total))
- Salad:
- 6 cups baby arugula
- 1 tablespoon extra virgin olive oil
- 1 tablespoon golden balsamic vinegar
- pinch salt
- black pepper

Directions:

1. Divide and arrange arugula on 4 salad plates or one platter.
2. Starting at the stem end, cut figs in half nearly through but leave the blossom end in tact.
3. Press 1/2 tablespoon cheese in the center then press halves back together. Wrap each fig with prosciutto half and secure with a toothpick.
4. GRILL: Preheat the grill to high heat, grill 5 minutes turning often until crisp. Remove and set aside.
5. AIR FRYER: Preheat the air fryer 400F 3 minutes. Air fry the figs 5 to 6 minutes, until crisp. Remove and set aside.
6. Place figs over arugula and drizzle with vinaigrette.

Notes:

1. You can prep them up to 1 day ahead and leave them refrigerated.

Grilled Watermelon Steaks

Ingredients:

- Watermelon Steaks
- Four 1-inch-thick watermelon wedges
- 2 Tbsp. extra-virgin olive oil
- 3/4 tsp garlic powder
- 1/2 tsp black pepper
- 1/2 tsp chili powder
- 1/4 tsp ground cumin
- 1/4 tsp ground coriander
- Arugula and Herb Salad
- 3 cups baby arugula
- 1/4 cup basil leaves
- 1/4 cup parsley leaves
- 1/4 cup mint leaves
- 1/3 cup extra-virgin olive oil
- Juice of 1 lemon
- Salt and black pepper
- 3 Tbsp. crumbled goat cheese

Directions:

1. In a small bowl, mix the spice rub by combining the garlic powder, pepper, chili powder, cumin and coriander.
2. Season each watermelon wedge with the spice mix and place on the preheated grill plate and grill until grill marks appear.
3. While the wedges are grilling, assemble the salad by mixing the arugula, basil, parsley, mint, olive oil, lemon juice, salt, pepper and crumbled goat cheese.
4. Serve the arugula and goat cheese salad with the grilled watermelon and enjoy by the pool!

Best Damn Air Fryer Pork Tenderloin

Servings: 4　　**Cooking Time:** 21 Mins.

Ingredients:

- Pork tenderloin (1.25lbs – 1.75lbs)
- 2 tbs brown sugar
- 1 tbs smoked paprika
- 1.5 tsp salt
- 1 tsp ground mustard
- 1/2 tsp onion powder
- 1/2 tsp ground black pepper
- 1/4 tsp garlic powder
- 1/4 tsp cayenne powder (optional)
- 1/2 tbs olive oil

Directions:

1. Mix all dry ingredients in a bowl.
2. Trim the pork tenderloin of any excess fat/silver skin. Coat with a 1/2 tablespoon olive oil. Rub spice mixture on entire pork tenderloin.
3. Preheat air fryer to 400° F for 5 minutes. After 5 minutes, carefully place pork tenderloin into air fryer and air fry at 400° F for 20-22 minutes. Internal temp should be 145° – 160° F.
4. When air fryer cycle is complete, carefully remove pork tenderloin to a cutting board and let rest for 5 minutes before slicing. Save any juices to serve over sliced meat.

Air-fryer Scotch Eggs

Servings: 6　　**Cooking Time:** 15 Mins.

Ingredients:

- 1 pound bulk pork sausage
- Salt and pepper to taste
- 6 hard-boiled large eggs
- 1 large egg, lightly beaten
- 3/4 cup crushed cornflakes

Directions:

1. Preheat air fryer to 400. Divide sausage into 6 portions; flatten and sprinkle with salt and pepper. Shape each portion around a peeled hard-boiled egg. Roll in beaten egg, then in cornflake crumbs.
2. Place in a single layer on greased tray in air-fryer basket. Cook until meat is no longer pink, turning halfway through, 12-15 minutes.

Air Fryer Steak

Servings: 4 **Cooking Time:** 10 Mins.

Ingredients:
- 4 sirloin steaks 4-6 oz each
- 2 tablespoons olive oil
- 1 teaspoon salt
- 1 teaspoon pepper

Directions:
1. Preheat the air fryer to 200C/400F.
2. Rub oil, salt, and pepper on the steaks.
3. Air fry the steaks for 10-12 minutes, flipping halfway through.
4. Let the steaks rest for 10 minutes.

Notes:
1. TO STORE: Place the steak and any excess juices in a shallow container and store it in the refrigerator for up to three days.
2. TO FREEZE: Place the cooked and cooled steak in an airtight container and store it in the freezer for up to 6 months.
3. TO REHEAT: Either microwave the steak for 20-30 seconds or reheat in a non-stick pan until hot.

Air Fryer Pork Chops

Cooking Time: 12 Mins.

Ingredients:
- 4 8-oz Pork chops (boneless or bone-in)
- 1 recipe Pork chop marinade (or 2 tbsp pork chop seasoning)

Directions:
1. Pat the pork chops dry with paper towels.
2. Prepare the pork chop marinade according to the instructions here. Marinate the pork chops for 1-12 hours (but not longer). (Alternatively, you can simply season generously with pork chop seasoning and skip the marinade, but the marinade makes them so juicy!)
3. Remove the chops from the fridge about 30 minutes before cooking.
4. Preheat the air fryer to 400 degrees F (204 degrees C) for 5 minutes.
5. Place pork chops in the air fryer basket in a single layer. Cook for about 12 minutes, flipping halfway through, until internal temperature reaches 145 degrees F (63 degrees C). Add an extra minute for bone-in pork chops.

Air Fryer Steak Bites

Servings: 4 **Cooking Time:** 6 Mins.

Ingredients:

- 1 lb steak ribeye or NY strip, cut into 1 inch cubes.
- 1 tablespoon oil
- 5 cloves garlic grated
- 1 teaspoon fresh ginger grated
- 1/3 cup low sodium soy sauce or tamari
- 1/4 cup honey
- 1 tablespoon toasted sesame oil
- 1 tablespoon rice vinegar
- For the Garnish
- sesame seeds
- sliced green onion

Directions:

1. To make the marinade: in a small mixing bowl add the garlic, ginger, soy sauce, honey, sesame oil, and rice vinegar. Whisk until well combined.
2. Add the cubed steak and marinade to a large zip-lock bag. Let marinade in the refrigerator for at least 30 minutes but up to 5 hours.
3. About 30 to 45 minutes before you plan on cooking, remove the zip-lock bag from the refrigerator and bring to room temperature.
4. With a pair of tongs, add the steak into the air fryer basket, discarding any of the excess marinade. (Do not empty the bag of juices into the air fryer basket!)
5. Cook at 400 F for 6 minutes, shaking the basket at the halfway mark.
6. Garnish with a sprinkle of sesame seeds and sliced green onion.

Notes:

1. It's best to cut the steak as uniformly as possible so the steak bites cook evenly in the air fryer.
2. You only need to shake the air fryer basket once. Shaking it too much will prevent a nice brown crust from forming on the steak.
3. If your air fryer basket is smaller, I suggest you air fry the steak bites in two batches. You want there to be some space between the steak in the basket. The beef will steam if you add too much to the basket.
4. Letting the air fried steak bites rest for a couple of minutes before serving will give the juices time to redistribute, and you'll have juicier steak bites.
5. These steak bites are scrumptious on their own. I also enjoy serving them with my crispy shallot green beans recipe, mushroom rice recipe, or air fryer potato wedges recipe! They're also great with some salad, pasta, or stir fried vegetables.
6. You can also add some chopped mushrooms or sliced onions to the marinade, and air fry them together.

Air Fryer Boneless Pork Chops

Servings: 4   **Cooking Time:** 10 Mins.

Ingredients:

- 4 boneless pork chops
- 1 tablespoon oil
- Salt and pepper to taste
- 1/2 cup of shredded parmesan cheese
- 2 tablespoons grated parmesan
- 1/2 teaspoon paprika
- 1/2 teaspoon garlic powder
- 1/2 teaspoon onion powder
- fresh parsley to garnish (optional)

Directions:

1. Preheat your air fryer to 380 degrees F.
2. Brush your pork chops with oil on both sides, then season one side with salt and pepper to taste.
3. Combine your parmesan cheeses with paprika, garlic powder, and onion powder.
4. Lay your pork chop in the parmesan mixture and coat both sides.
5. Place your pork chops in the air fryer basket in a single layer so they are not touching. Cook for 9 to 10 minutes (internal temperature for pork chops should reach 145 degrees), flipping halfway through.

Notes:

1. If you have thin slices of pork chops it will vary a few minutes less, and thicker will vary a few minutes more.
2. HOW TO COOK FROZEN BONELESS PORK CHOPS IN THE AIR FRYER:
3. Preheat your air fryer to 380 degrees F.
4. Once preheated, lay the frozen pork chops in the air fryer basket, making sure they're not touching.
5. Cook for 12 to 18 minutes, flipping halfway through.
6. HOW TO REHEAT BONELESS PORK CHOPS IN THE AIR FRYER:
7. Preheat the air fryer to 350 degrees F.
8. Once preheated, lay the leftover pork chops in the basket in a single layer.
9. Cook for 3 to 5 minutes until warmed through.

BREAKFAST & BRUNCH RECIPES

Air-fryer Falafel Wraps Recipe

Servings: 2   **Cooking Time:** 15 Mins.

Ingredients:

- ½ red onion, thinly sliced
- 4 tbsp white wine vinegar
- 2 plain Laffa-style flatbreads or large white bread wraps
- 100g red pepper houmous
- 1 salad tomato, sliced
- 30g sliced gherkins
- 2 green pickled chillies (optional)
- For the falafel
- 400g tin chickpeas in water, liquid reserved
- 5g coriander, torn
- zest of ½ lemon
- ½ small red onion, chopped
- 1 tbsp sesame seeds
- 2 cloves garlic, roughly chopped
- ½ tsp ground coriander
- ½ tsp salt
- sunflower oil spray

Directions:

1. Preheat the air-fryer to 200°C.
2. Put all the ingredients for the falafel, except the oil, into the bowl of a food processor and pulse until finely chopped. Add 2-3 tbsp of the reserved chickpea liquid, and blend until the mixture is sticking together.
3. Divide the mixture into 8 and press gently into patties.
4. Spray the air-fryer basket with sunflower oil and place the falafels in a single layer. Spray the tops with more oil and cook for 15 mins until crisp and browned.
5. Meanwhile, put the sliced red onion into a small bowl along with the vinegar and a pinch of salt. Leave to pickle for 10 mins, then drain.
6. To assemble, lay the flatbreads or wraps out and spread thickly with the houmous. Top with the crisp falafels and heap on the pickled onions, sliced tomatoes and gherkins. Add a pickled chilli, if you like, and serve while warm.

Breakfast Sliders

Servings: 6   **Cooking Time:** 5 Mins.

Ingredients:

- 4 eggs
- 2 tablespoons milk
- ⅛ teaspoon salt
- ⅛ teaspoon pepper
- 6 Hawaiian rolls half pack
- 3 large slices ham cut in half
- 3 slices cheese American, Swiss, etc.
- 2 tablespoons butter melted
- 1 tablespoon everything bagel seasoning

Directions:

1. In a microwave-safe bowl, whisk together eggs, milk, salt, and pepper.
2. Microwave the egg mixture in 45-second increments, stirring after each time, until firm but still moist. This should take about 2 1/2 minutes total.
3. On the bottom half of each roll, add a folded slice of ham. Top with scrambled eggs and cheese, and cover with the top half of the rolls.
4. In a small bowl, mix melted butter and everything bagel seasoning. Brush over the rolls.
5. Place the rolls in the basket of an air fryer and cook at 300°F for 5-8 minutes, until the cheese is melted and the tops are golden.
6. Serve while hot.

Air Fryer, herb Butter Dinner Rolls

Servings: 8   **Cooking Time:** 5 Mins.

Ingredients:

- 8 rolls frozen
- 1/4 cup butter melted, unsalted
- 2 tablspoons Italian seasoning

Directions:

1. Spread the frozen rolls onto the baking sheet or in the air fryer basket.
2. In a small bowl, mix the melted butter with the herbs.
3. Brush on the butter and herb mixture onto the rolls.
4. Set in the air fryer at 320 degrees F, for 5 minutes.
5. Plate, serve and enjoy!

Air-fryer Scones

Servings: 12 **Cooking Time:** 30 Mins.

Ingredients:

- 3 1/2 cups self-raising flour, plus extra for dusting
- 1 cup thickened cream
- 1 cup lemonade
- 5ml olive oil cooking spray
- 1/2 cup strawberry jam
- 1/2 cup double thick cream

Directions:

1. Preheat air fryer to 170°C for 3 minutes. Place flour in a large bowl. Make a well in the centre. Add thickened cream and lemonade. Using a flat-bladed knife, stir until a sticky dough forms. Turn dough out onto a lightly floured surface and knead until just smooth (don't over-knead).
2. Flatten dough until 5cm-thick. Using a 6cm-round cutter, cut out scones. Press leftover dough together and repeat to make a total of 12 scones.
3. Pull out air-fryer pan and basket, then spray basket with oil. Place 6 scones, side by side, in basket. Slide pan and basket into air fryer. Set timer for 15 minutes and cook until light golden and hollow when tapped on top. Repeat with remaining scones. Serve with jam and cream.

Air Fryer Breakfast Potatoes

Servings: 4 **Cooking Time:** 20 Mins.

Ingredients:

- 4 Russet Potatoes Cut into cubes
- 2 tbsp olive oil
- 1 tsp salt
- 1 tsp garlic powder
- 1 tsp paprika
- 1/2 tsp black pepper

Directions:

1. Peel, rinse, and then cut the potatoes into 1 inch cubes, about the size of dice.
2. Next, using a mixing bowl, toss the cubed potatoes in olive oil and then the seasonings, until they are well coated.
3. Place the seasoned potatoes in the air fryer basket, and air fry at 400 degrees F for 20 minutes, shaking the basket halfway through the cooking time.
4. The potatoes should be golden brown and crispy when done.
5. Serve while hot.

Air Fryer Falafel

Servings: 20

Ingredients:

- 1/2 yellow onion, cut into quarters
- 1/4 c. packed cilantro leaves
- 1/4 c. packed parlsey leaves
- 4 cloves garlic
- 2 (15-oz.) cans chickpeas, rinsed and drained
- 2 tsp. ground cumin
- 1 tsp. baking powder
- 1 tsp. dried coriander
- 1 tsp. kosher salt, plus more
- 1/2 tsp. crushed red pepper flakes, plus more
- 1/3 c. tahini
- Juice of 1/2 lemon
- 3 tbsp. (or more) water

Directions:

1. In a food processor, pulse onion, cilantro, parsley, and garlic, scraping down sides, until roughly chopped. Add chickpeas, cumin, baking powder, coriander, 1 teaspoon salt, and 1/2 teaspoon red pepper flakes. Pulse until chickpeas are mostly broken down with some chunks; stop just before mixture turns into a paste. Taste and adjust seasonings.
2. Scoop out about 2 tablespoons chickpea mixture and gently form into a ball without squeezing too much or falafel will be dense. Working in batches, in an air-fryer basket, arrange balls. Cook at 370° until browned, about 15 minutes.
3. Meanwhile, in a medium bowl, combine tahini and lemon juice. Add water and stir until combined, adding more water 1 tablespoon at a time until desired consistency is reached; season with salt and red pepper flakes.
4. Serve falafel as is with sauce, in a salad, or in a pita.

Air Fryer Taco Shells

Servings: 4 **Cooking Time:** 4 Mins.

Ingredients:

- 4 corn tortillas
- 1 tablespoon olive oil or avocado oil

Directions:

1. Use a pastry brush and lightly coat each tortilla with oil on both sides.
2. Drape the shell over the taco mold. Place mold in the air fryer basket. If you don't have the molds, you can use aluminum foil to make small tents to lay the tortillas over as they cook.
3. Air fry at 400 degrees F for 4-6 minutes until golden and crisp. (Check after two minutes as the fan may shift the tortilla.)
4. Fill with your favorite toppings.

Notes:

1. Optional Favorite Taco Toppings: Sour cream, hot sauce, layer of a favorite cheese, nacho cheese, fresh squeeze of lime or lemon, homemade coleslaw, diced tomatoes, salsa, chopped onion, creamy guacamole or crisp romaine lettuce.
2. Optional Favorite Taco Fillings: Seasoned ground beef, black beans, shredded chicken, grilled carne asada, crispy fried fish or blackened Portobello mushrooms.
3. Substitutions: Use non-stick cooking spray, avocado oil spray or olive oil cooking spray if you do not have any bottled oils. If you prefer flour tortillas, you can use them instead of the corn, cooking time may need to be adjusted to get them crispy.

Texas Toast In The Air Fryer

Servings: 4 **Cooking Time:** 10 Mins.

Ingredients:

- 4 slices Texas Toast, frozen or fresh

Directions:

1. Place the Texas Toast slices into the basket in a single layer, so they are not overlapping.
2. FOR FROZEN TOAST air fry at 350 degrees F for 8-10 minutes, flipping the slices halfway through the cooking time.
3. FOR FROZEN CHEESE TOAST, air fry at 350 degrees F for 6-10 minutes without flipping until the cheese is melted and golden.
4. FOR FRESH TOAST, air fry at 350 degrees F for 4-5 minutes, flipping the slices halfway through the cooking time.

Air-fryer Breakfast Burritos

Servings: 4

Ingredients:
- 6 medium flour tortillas
- 6 scrambled eggs
- ½ lb ground sausage – browned
- ½ bell pepper – minced
- ⅓ cup bacon bits
- ½ cup shredded cheese
- oil for spraying

Directions:
1. Combine the scrambled eggs, cooked sausage, bell pepper, bacon bits, and cheese in a large bowl. Stir to combine.
2. Spoon about a ½ cup of the mixture into the center of a flour tortilla.
3. Fold in the sides & then roll.
4. Repeat with the remaining ingredients.
5. Place the filled burritos into the air fryer basket & spray liberally with oil.
6. Cook at 330 degrees for 5 minutes or until hot and the tortilla is slightly cripsy.

Air-fryer Garlic Bread

Servings: 8

Ingredients:
- 1/4 cup butter, softened
- 3 tablespoons grated Parmesan cheese
- 2 garlic cloves, minced
- 2 teaspoons minced fresh parsley or 1/2 teaspoon dried parsley flakes
- 8 slices ciabatta or French bread

Directions:
1. Preheat air fryer to 350°. In a small bowl, combine first 4 ingredients; spread over bread.
2. In batches, arrange bread in a single layer on tray in air-fryer basket. Cook until golden brown, 2-3 minutes. Serve warm.

DESSERTS RECIPES

Air-fryer Healthier Apple Chips

Servings: 2 **Cooking Time: 30 Mins.**

Ingredients:
- 5ml olive oil cooking spray
- 1 Pink Lady apple, cut into 1mm-thick slices
- 1/2 tsp cinnamon sugar

Directions:
1. Preheat air fryer to 180°C for 2 minutes. Lightly spray air-fryer basket with oil.
2. Place apple in a medium bowl. Sprinkle with sugar and toss to combine.
3. Working in 3 batches, cook apple in air fryer for 10 minutes or until dehydrated, separating slightly halfway through cooking. Stand for 5 minutes to allow to crisp, then serve.

Air Fryer Apple Crumble

Servings: 6-8 **Cooking Time: 25 Mins.**

Ingredients:
- 2 large Bramley apples
- 250g plain flour
- 1 tsp ground cinnamon
- 150g butter
- 75g brown sugar

Directions:
1. Peel and chop the apples into small chunks and place them in an air fryer safe baking tin. Sprinkle 2 tablespoons of water over the top of them.
2. Air fryer at 180°C for 15 minutes, or until the apple chunks soften.
3. While the apples are in the air fryer, you can make the crumble mixture. In a mixing bowl, combine the flour and butter. Using your hands, rub it together until it resembles breadcrumbs and then add the sugar and ground cinnamon, stirring it in. Alternatively, you can use a food processor but be careful not to over-process; the crumble needs to have enough texture and not be too fine.
4. When the apples are ready, add the crumble mixture on top.
5. Close the air fryer basket and continue to air fry at the same temperature for a further 10 minutes, checking on it to make sure it isn't burning. When the crumble is crispy and golden, it is ready.
6. Tastes great with custard or ice cream.

Notes:
1. Instead of using the air fryer, you can also soften the apples in a pan and some water on the stove.

Air Fryer Apricot And Raisin Cake

Servings: 8   Cooking Time: 12 Mins.

Ingredients:

- 75g dried apricots, (just under 1/2 cup)
- 4 tbsp orange juice
- 75g self-raising flour, (3/4 cup)
- 40 g Sugar, (1/3 cup)
- 1 egg
- 75g Raisins, (just under 1/2 a cup)

Directions:

1. Preheat air fryer to 160C/320F
2. In a blender or food processor blend the dried apricots and juice until they are smooth.
3. In a separate bowl, mix together the sugar and flour.
4. Beat the egg. Add it to the flour and sugar. Mix together.
5. Add the apricot puree and raisins. Combine together.
6. Spray an air fryer safe baking tin with a little oil. Transfer the mixture over and level off.
7. Cook in the air fryer for 12 minutes, check it at 10 minutes. Use a metal skewer to see if it is done. If need be, return the cake to the air fryer to cook for a few more minutes to brown up.
8. Allow to cool before removing from the baking tin and slicing up.

Baked Corn And Crab Cakes

Servings: 8   Cooking Time: 30 Mins.

Ingredients:

- 1 cup corn kernels (fresh)
- 1 cup about 30 reduced-fat Ritz crackers, crushed
- 1 whole egg plus 2 egg whites (beaten)
- 4 scallions (chopped fine)
- 1/4 cup minced red bell pepper
- 2 tbsp light mayonnaise
- 2 tbsp fat free yogurt
- 1/4 cup fresh parsley
- 1 lemon (juiced)
- 16 oz premium lump crab meat (picked free of shells)
- salt and pepper to taste
- cooking spray

Directions:

1. In a large bowl, combine corn, crushed crackers, eggs, scallions, pepper, mayo, yogurt, parsley, lemon juice, salt and pepper.
2. Mix well, then fold in crab meat, careful not to over mix so the crab remains in large chunks.
3. Gently shape into 8 patties using a 1/2 cup measuring cup.
4. Chill in the refrigerator at least 1 hour before baking.
5. Preheat oven to 425F. Grease a baking sheet with cooking spray.
6. Bake about 24 to 28 minutes turning halfway, or until golden brown.
7. Air Fryer Directions:
8. Air fry, in batches 370F until the edges are golden, about 10 to 12 minutes turning halfway.

Notes:

1. The trick to making sure the crab cakes hold together is to refrigerate them before baking, so don't skip that step.

Air Fryer Lava Cakes

Servings: 2 **Cooking Time:** 10 Mins.

Ingredients:
- 1/2 cup semi-sweet chocolate chips
- 4 tablespoons butter
- 2 eggs
- 1 teaspoon vanilla extract
- 1/4 teaspoon salt
- 3 tablespoons all-purpose flour
- 1/2 cup powdered sugar
- FOR THE NUTELLA FILLING
- 2 tablespoons Nutella
- 1 tablespoon butter, softened
- 1 tablespoon powdered sugar

Directions:
1. Preheat your air fryer to 370 degrees.
2. In a medium microwave-safe bowl, add the chocolate chips and butter and heat on 30-second increments until completely melted and smooth, stirring during each interval.
3. Add the eggs, vanilla, salt, flour, and powdered sugar to the bowl and whisk to combine.
4. In a separate bowl, mix the Nutella, softened butter, and powdered sugar.
5. Prepare the ramekins by spraying them with oil and fill each one-half full with the chocolate chip mixture. Add half of the Nutella filling in the center of each ramekin, then top off with the remaining chocolate chip mixture making sure the Nutella is covered.
6. Carefully place the lava cakes into the air fryer and cook for 8 to 11 minutes.
7. Carefully remove the lava cakes from the air fryer and allow them to cool for 5 minutes. Take a butterknife and run around the outside edges of the cake and flip out onto a serving plate.
8. Top with ice cream, chocolate syrup and/or other toppings and enjoy!

Notes:
1. HOW TO MAKE FROZEN LAVA CAKES IN THE AIR FRYER:
2. Preheat your air fryer to 350 degrees.
3. Transfer the frozen lava cake into an oven-safe ramekin and cook for 10-12 minutes.
4. Flip the lava cake onto a plate, let cool for a few minutes, add toppings, then enjoy!

Air Fryer Cheesecake Recipe

Servings: 8   **Cooking Time:** 22 Mins.

Ingredients:

- 1 1/2 cups graham crackers
- 14 oz sweetened condensed milk
- 1/2 cup salted butter melted
- 2 eggs
- 1 tsp vanilla
- 24 oz cream cheese room temperature
- 1 can cherry pie filling

Directions:

1. Take the graham crackers and add them to a food processor. Continue to blend and pulse until they are finely crushed. Place into a small mixing bowl.
2. Add the melted butter to the graham crackers and mix until fully combined. Set aside.
3. Add butter to the bottom and sides of the 7" Springform pan. Place a piece of parchment paper on the bottom of the pan.
4. Press the graham cracker mixture into the bottom of the pan. Use a spoon to press the graham cracker crust down firmly.
5. In a medium mixing bowl, use a hand mixer or a stand mixer on medium speed to blend the room temperature cream cheese until creamy and smooth. Add the eggs, condensed milk, and vanilla to the cream cheese and blend on medium speed until the mixture is completely smooth. About 2 minutes.
6. Pour the cream cheese mixture over the graham cracker crust. It will fill almost completely up to the rim of the 7" cheesecake pan.
7. Carefully place the springform pan into the basket of the Air Fryer. (You do not preheat the Air Fryer for this recipe).
8. Bake in the Air Fryer at 300 degrees Fahrenheit for 20-22 minutes, or until the center is no longer jiggling. (It will still wiggle, but won't be a wet jiggle.) If needed, continue to add 2 minutes increments at 300 degrees Fahrenheit until the center is perfect.
9. Carefully remove the springform pan from the Air Fryer basket and allow it to chill in the refrigerator for 6-8 hours, or overnight.
10. Once chilled, carefully remove the circular sides of the springform pan and place the cheesecake on a serving platter. Top with the cherry pie filling just before slicing and serving.

Notes:

1. Make sure to grease the sides and bottom of the springform pan so that the cheesecake does not stick to the sides when you go to remove the sides of the pan.
2. Place parchment paper at the bottom of the buttered springform pan.
3. If the cheesecake still looks wet and jiggly in the center after 20-22 minutes, continue to add 2 minute increments at 300 degrees Fahrenheit to completely cook. NOTE: It will still have a little wiggle to it, but won't look wet.
4. Allow the pan to cool slightly before carefully removing it from the Air Fryer basket.
5. Give the cheesecake 6-8 hours, or overnight to completely chill and set.
6. Add the cherry topping just before slicing and serving the cheesecake.
7. Store the cheesecake in an airtight container in the refrigerator for up to 3 days.
8. If using an 8" Springform pan, increase the graham crackers to 2 cups with the ½ cup butter to fill the bottom of the 8" pan. You will bake at 300 degrees Fahrenheit for 15 minutes, and add 2 minute increments when using an 8" pan.

Air Fried Mac N Cheese Balls

Ingredients:

- 4 cups of leftover mac and cheese
- 1.5 cups of seasoned breadcrumbs (see below for substitutions)
- 1 egg
- 1 Tbsp. milk
- Vegetable Oil

Directions:

1. In a bowl, beat 1 egg and add milk. Mix well.
2. In a separate bowl, add seasoned breadcrumbs.
3. Cut leftover mac and cheese into balls.
4. Dip each ball into egg and bread crumbs.
5. Place in air fryer. Brush with olive oil.
6. Cook at 370F for 5-8 minutes.
7. Shake and brush with more oil.
8. Cook for an additional 2 minutes.
9. Optional: serve with marinara sauce.

Air Fryer Frozen Waffles

Servings: 1   Cooking Time: 6 Mins.

Ingredients:

- 2 Frozen Waffles
- optional toppings (syrup, berries, whipped cream, jam, etc.)

Directions:

1. Place the frozen waffles in the air fryer basket and spread in an even layer (make sure they aren't overlapping). No oil spray is needed.
2. Air Fry at 360°F/180°C for 4 minutes. Flip the waffles over.
3. Continue to Air Fry at 360°F/180°C for another 1-3 minutes or until to your preferred doneness.
4. Serve with your favorite toppings.

Notes:

1. No Oil Necessary. Cook Frozen - Do not thaw first.
2. Cook in a single layer in the air fryer basket.
3. Recipe timing is based on a non-preheated air fryer. If cooking in multiple batches back to back, the following batches may cook a little quicker.
4. Recipes were tested in 3.7 to 6 qt. air fryers. If using a larger air fryer, they might cook quicker so adjust cooking time.

Italian Pastries With Creamy Semolina Filling

Servings: 18   **Cooking Time:** 14 Mins.

Ingredients:

- 2 cups whole milk
- ½ cup granulated sugar
- ¼ teaspoon kosher salt
- 1 cup semolina flour
- 1 ½ cups ricotta cheese
- ½ cup heavy cream
- 1 lemon, zested and juiced
- 1 teaspoon ground cinnamon
- ½ teaspoon ground fennel seeds
- 2 sheet frozen puff pastry sheets, thawed
- 1 ½ cups ricotta cheese
- ½ cup heavy cream
- Items Needed
- Rolling pin
- Pastry brush
- 18 silicone or cardboard cupcake liners

Directions:

1. Place the milk, sugar, and salt into a medium saucepan over medium heat and whisk together, then bring to a simmer.
2. Slowly whisk in the semolina to the milk mixture until it is thickened and smooth, then transfer the mixture into a large bowl and stir in the ricotta, cream, lemon zest, lemon juice, cinnamon, and ground fennel seeds, and one egg.
3. Roll out the puff pastry to 1/8-inch thickness using a rolling pin, then cut it in to 9 pieces and lay each piece into a cupcake liner. Press the center of the dough into the liner, leaving the corners hanging over the edge.
4. Place 2 tablespoons of filling into the center of each dough piece and fold the four corners over it so they meet in the center.
5. Beat together the remaining egg and 1 tablespoon of water, then brush the top of each pastry with the egg wash and sprinkle with a bit of demerara sugar.
6. Place the crisper plate into the Smart Air Fryer basket.
7. Place 6 of the pastries onto the crisper plate.
8. Select the Bake function, adjust the temperature to 340°F and time to 14 minutes, and press Start/Pause.
9. Remove the pastries when done, let cool for 5 minutes, then serve. Repeat the baking process as needed with remaining pastries.

Fried Oreos

Ingredients:

- 9 Oreo cookies
- 1 Crescent sheet roll
- desired toppings

Directions:

1. Pop the crescent sheet roll and spread it on the table. Line and cut 9 even squares with a knife.
2. Get your Oreo cookies and wrap them in the squares.
3. Place your prepared cookies in the air fryer basket lined with perforated parchment paper (optional). Air fry at 360°F for 2 minutes. Flip them over and cook for another 2 minutes.
4. Sprinkle with powdered sugar or cinnamon and pair with your favorite dipping sauce and enjoy!

SNACKS & APPETIZERS RECIPES

Air Fryer Wontons

Servings: 30 **Cooking Time:** 20 Mins.

Ingredients:

- 250g pork mince
- 150g prawn meat, diced
- 1/2 tbsp finely grated fresh ginger
- 2 garlic cloves, crushed
- 1 tbsp finely chopped green shallots
- 1 tbsp light soy sauce
- 2 tsp caster sugar
- 1 tsp salt
- 1 egg, lightly beaten
- 30 gow gee wrappers
- Honey sesame dipping sauce
- 2 tbsp light soy sauce
- 1 tbsp Chinese rice wine
- 1 tsp sesame oil
- 1 tbsp honey
- 1 tsp toasted sesame seeds
- Select all ingredients

Directions:

1. To make the dipping sauce, combine all ingredients in a bowl and set aside.
2. Combine the pork, prawn, ginger, shallot, garlic, soy, sugar and salt in a bowl. Place 1 tsp mixture in the centre of a wonton wrapper. Brush edge with egg and fold over wrapper to seal. Pinch edge together to make a wonton shape. Repeat with the remaining mixture and wrappers.
3. Place half the wontons in an air fryer basket and spray with oil. Air fry at 180C for 10 minutes. Repeat with remaining wontons.
4. Serve hot with little bowls of dipping sauce on the side.

Roasted Green Beans

Servings: 2 **Cooking Time:** 10 Mins.

Ingredients:

- 1 pound green beans, trimmed
- 2 tablespoons Dijon mustard
- 2 tablespoons olive oil
- 2 teaspoon red wine vinegar
- 1 garlic clove, minced
- 1 teaspoon salt
- 1 teaspoon pepper

Directions:

1. Select the Preheat function on the Air Fryer, then press Start/Pause.
2. Place the ingredients into a large bowl and toss together until the green beans are well coated.
3. Place the green beans into the preheated air fryer basket.
4. Set the temperature to 380°F, adjust the time to 10 minutes, then press Start/Pause.
5. Shake the basket halfway through the cooking time.
6. Remove the green beans when done and serve.

Jicama Fries In The Air Fryer

Servings: 6   **Cooking Time:** 28 Mins.

Ingredients:

- 8 cups Jicama (peeled and cut into fries, about 1/3 to 1/2 inch thick and 3 to 4 inches long)
- 2 tbsp Olive oil
- 1/2 tsp Garlic powder
- 1 tsp Cumin
- 1 tsp Sea salt
- 1/4 tsp Black pepper

Directions:

1. Boil a large pot of water on the stove. Add the jicama fries and boil for 18 to 25 minutes, until color becomes slightly translucent (instead of bright white) and no longer crunchy. Time will vary depending on the thickness of your fries.
2. When the jicama is not crunchy anymore, remove and pat dry.
3. Set the air fryer oven to 400 degrees (204 degrees C) and let it preheat for 2 to 3 minutes.
4. Place the fries into a large bowl. Drizzle with olive oil and season with garlic powder, cumin, and sea salt. Toss to coat.
5. Working in batches to avoid crowding, arrange jicama in the air fryer basket in a single layer, preferably with the pieces not touching each other. Air fry jicama fries for 10-12 minutes, until golden. Repeat with remaining fries.

Frozen Onion Rings In Air Fryer

Servings: 4   **Cooking Time:** 8 Mins.

Ingredients:

- 1 Bag Frozen Onion Rings

Directions:

1. Spray basket with nonstick cooking spray such as an olive oil spray on the basket to help with clean up. Grab your favorite brand of frozen onion rings. Open package and in a single layer, place the onion rings in the air fryer basket.
2. Air fry at 380 degrees f for 8-10 minutes, flip halfway through air frying. For crispier onion rings, add an additional 1-2 minutes additional time.
3. Remove from basket with tongs and serve with your favorite sauce.

Notes:

1. Try not to overfill the basket, so air fry onion rings in batches if necessary.

Air Fryer Greek Crescent Nachos

Servings: 6

Ingredients:

- 1 can (8 oz) refrigerated Pillsbury™ Original Crescent Dough Sheet or 1 can (8 oz) refrigerated Pillsbury™ Original Crescent Rolls (8 Count)
- 1/2 teaspoon Greek seasoning
- 1/2 cup tzatziki yogurt dip (from 8- to 12-oz tub)
- 4 oz feta cheese, crumbled
- 1/2 cup grape or cherry tomatoes, quartered
- 1/2 cup chopped cucumber
- 1 tablespoon finely chopped red onion
- Fresh dill weed, if desired

Directions:

1. If using dough sheet: Unroll dough; press into 12x8-inch rectangle. Sprinkle with Greek seasoning. Cut in half lengthwise, then in sixths crosswise. Cut each smaller rectangle in half diagonally to make 24 triangles. If using crescent rolls: Unroll dough; separate into 8 triangles; cut each into 3 smaller triangles, to make 24 triangles (triangles will be shaped slightly differently).
2. Spray 5.8- to 6-quart air fryer basket with cooking spray. Arrange 8 dough triangles in air fryer. Set air fryer to 380°F; cook 2 to 4 minutes or until golden brown. Repeat twice with remaining crescent triangles.
3. Arrange chips on platter; spoon tzatziki yogurt dip over chips, spreading slightly. Top with feta cheese, tomatoes, cucumber, onion and dill weed.

Air Fryer Pasta Chips

Servings: 8 **Cooking Time:** 40 Mins.

Ingredients:
- 2 cups farfalle pasta
- 1 tablespoon olive oil
- ½ cup grated Parmesan cheese
- 1 teaspoon garlic powder
- 1 teaspoon Italian seasoning
- ½ teaspoon salt

Directions:
1. Bring a large pot of lightly salted water to a boil; add pasta and cook, stirring occasionally, until tender yet firm to the bite, about 8 minutes. Drain, but do not rinse. Let sit for 2 minutes.
2. Preheat an air fryer to 400 degrees F (200 degrees C).
3. Meanwhile, transfer pasta to a large bowl and drizzle with olive oil; stir in Parmesan cheese, garlic powder, Italian seasoning, and salt until evenly combined. Arrange 1/4 of the pasta in a single layer in the air fryer basket.
4. Cook in the preheated air fryer for 5 minutes; flip and cook 2 to 3 minutes more. Transfer to a paper towel-lined plate and break apart any pasta chips that have stuck together; let cool completely. Repeat with remaining pasta.

Notes:
1. All air fryers are not created equal. Mine is just under 4 quarts and I was able to fit 1/4 of the pasta at one time.

Air Fryer Zucchini Chips

Servings: 2-4 **Cooking Time:** 14-16 Mins.

Ingredients:
- FOR THE ZUCCHINI CHIPS:
- 1 medium zucchini (about 8 ounces)
- 1/2 teaspoon kosher salt
- Cooking spray
- 2 tablespoons grated Parmesan cheese (about 1/2 ounce), divided
- 1/2 teaspoon garlic powder, divided
- FOR THE HERBY YOGURT DIPPING SAUCE:
- 1 small clove garlic
- 2 teaspoons finely chopped fresh basil leaves, plus more for serving
- 1/4 cup plain whole-milk or 2% yogurt
- 1/2 teaspoon grated Parmesan cheese
- Pinch kosher salt
- Freshly ground black pepper

Directions:
1. Using a mandoline or sharp knife, cut 1 medium zucchini crosswise into very thin rounds about 1/8-inch thick. Toss with 1/2 teaspoon kosher salt in a bowl, spread them out in a single layer on a double layer of paper towels to dry, then set aside for 5 to 10 minutes.
2. Finely grate 1 small garlic clove into a small bowl. Finely chop 2 teaspoons fresh basil leaves and add to the bowl. Add 1/4 cup plain yogurt, 1/2 teaspoon grated Parmesan cheese, a pinch of kosher salt, and a few grinds of black pepper. Stir to combine. Garnish with more chopped basil leaves, if desired.
3. Heat an air fryer to 370°F. Pat the tops of the zucchini slices dry with paper towels. Coat the air fryer basket or tray with cooking spray. Add enough zucchini slices to sit in a single, even layer. Coat with cooking spray, then sprinkle with 1 tablespoon of the grated Parmesan cheese and 1/4 teaspoon of the garlic powder. Air-fry until golden-brown, 7 to 8 minutes. Check the chips halfway through: Smaller chips may brown and crisp before larger ones, so remove those that are ready with tongs.
4. Carefully transfer the chips with a slotted spoon or tongs to a serving plate or bowl. Repeat air frying the remaining chips, patting them dry before placing in the air frying if needed. Serve immediately with the dipping sauce.

Notes:
1. Make ahead: Herby yogurt sauce can be made up to 2 days in advance and refrigerated in an airtight container.
2. Storage: Air fryer zucchini chips are best eaten the day they are made. Leftovers can be stored in an airtight container at room temperature and reheated in the air fryer for 2 minutes to re-crisp.

Air Fryer Kale Chips

Ingredients:

- 1 lb. kale
- 1 tbsp. olive oil or avocado oil
- sea salt to taste

Directions:

1. Rinse kale and dry thoroughly.
2. Cut kale leaves from stem and make into bite sized pieces.
3. Place in a large bowl and toss with oil and salt.
4. Place 1/4 of the kale inside the air fryer basket and air fryer at 400F for 3 minutes. Repeat until kale is cooked.
5. Enjoy!

Poutine

Servings: 4   **Cooking Time:** 30 Mins.

Ingredients:

- 5 large potatoes, peeled and sliced into chunky chips
- 1 tbs olive oil
- 1 tbs butter
- 1 large onion, peeled and finely sliced
- 1 tbs plain flour
- 1 3/4 cup beef stock, made with 1 stock cube
- 250g mozzarella, torn

Directions:

1. Rinse the chips and dry with a tea towel. Place the potatoes in the air fryer basket, drizzle with oil and toss well.
2. Cook for 25 minutes at 180°C, tossing halfway through. Check the chips after 25 minutes and cook for 5 minutes more, or until crisp and golden.
3. Heat the butter in a saucepan on medium heat and cook the onion for 12-15 minutes, stirring, until soft. Sprinkle over the flour and cook for 1 minute.
4. Gradually add the stock, stirring all the time. Cook for 5 more minutes until thick and bubbling.
5. Divide the chips between 4 dishes, pour gravy on top, dot with torn mozzarella and serve.

Air Fryer Green Beans

Servings: 4 **Cooking Time:** 10 Mins.

Ingredients:

- 1 pound fresh green beans or haricots verts
- 2 teaspoons extra-virgin olive oil
- 1/2 teaspoon kosher salt
- 1/2 teaspoon garlic powder optional
- 1/4 teaspoon ground black pepper or red pepper flakes
- 3 tablespoons freshly grated Parmesan cheese optional for serving
- Lemon wedges optional for serving

Directions:

1. Rinse the green beans and pat VERY dry. Trim off the ends and halve any longer beans so that all of the pieces are roughly the same length.
2. Place the green beans in a large mixing bowl. Top with the oil, salt, garlic powder (if using), and black pepper. Toss to thoroughly and evenly coat the beans with the oil and seasonings.
3. Preheat the air fryer to 375°F. Add half of the green beans in a single layer (it's OK if they touch, but you don't want the layer to be thick; for most air fryers, two batches will do it.)
4. Air fry for 8 to 10 minutes, tossing halfway through, until the green beans are crisp-tender and dark in spots (if you like your green beans with more bite, cook on the shorter end of the time; for more char but a slightly softer bean, cook them for the full 10 minutes). If desired, transfer to a sheet pan and place in a 200°F oven to keep them warm while you cook the second batch. Repeat with the remaining green beans.
5. Transfer to a serving plate. Sprinkle generously with the Parmesan. Serve immediately, with lemon wedges squeezed over the top as desired.

Notes:

1. TO STORE: Refrigerate green beans in an airtight storage container for up to 4 days.
2. TO REHEAT: Rewarm leftovers in the air fryer at 350°F for about 5 minutes, tossing once halfway through. You can also rewarm beans in the microwave.
3. TO FREEZE: Freeze leftovers in an airtight, freezer-safe storage container for up to 3 months. Let thaw overnight in the refrigerator before reheating.

FAVORITE AIR FRYER RECIPES

Air Fryer Fried Ravioli On A Stick

Servings: 4　　**Cooking Time:** Mins.

Ingredients:

- 1 cup All-purpose flour
- 2 eggs
- 1 cup breadcrumbs
- 1/2 cup grated Parmesan cheese, plus more for sprinkling
- 2 tablespoons dried oregano
- 1 teaspoon dried thyme
- 3 teaspoons 's House Seasoning
- 12 frozen 4-cheese ravioli, thawed
- olive oil, for spraying
- 1/2 cup pesto, for dipping
- 4 bamboo skewers, soaked in water

Directions:

1. Place flour in a medium bowl. In a small bowl, beat eggs. In a shallow dish, mix breadcrumbs, 1/2 cup of the Parmesan cheese, oregano, thyme, and House Seasoning.
2. Add ravioli to flour, toss to coat, and gently shake off excess. Dip each ravioli in egg, shaking off excess. Roll each ravioli gently in breadcrumb mixture. On a skewer, thread 3 breaded ravioli. Spray both sides with oil.
3. Working in batches of 4, place skewers in air fryer basket. Set temperature to 400 degrees, and air fry for 4 minutes. Turn skewers, spray with oil, and air fry for 2 minutes more. Repeat with remaining skewers. Sprinkle with Parmesan cheese, and serve warm with warm pesto on the side.

Air Fryer Taquitos Recipe

Servings: 4-6   **Cooking Time:** 15-30 Mins.

Ingredients:

- FOR THE TAQUITOS:
- 6 ounces cream cheese
- 1 canned chipotle pepper in adobo sauce
- 1 teaspoon canned chipotle in adobo sauce
- 1 (4-ounce) can mild diced green chiles
- 1 teaspoon chili powder
- 1 teaspoon ground cumin
- 3/4 teaspoon kosher salt
- 12 ounces cooked boneless chicken (about 3 cups, from 1 rotisserie chicken)
- 4 ounces shredded Mexican blend cheese (about 1 cup)
- 14 to 16 (5 to 6-inch) corn or flour tortillas, divided
- Cooking spray
- 14 to 16 toothpicks
- SERVING OPTIONS:
- Guacamole
- Sour cream or crema
- Avocado crema
- Shredded iceberg lettuce
- Diced tomatoes

Directions:

1. Place 6 ounces cream cheese in a large microwave-safe bowl. Microwave on high until softened but not melted, 15 to 20 seconds. (Alternatively, let sit at room temperature until softened.)
2. Finely chop 1 canned chipotle in adobo sauce (about 1 tablespoon). Add the chipotle, 1 teaspoon of the sauce, 1 (4-ounce) can mild diced green chiles (do not drain), 1 teaspoon chili powder, 1 teaspoon ground cumin, and 3/4 teaspoon kosher salt to the cream cheese. Stir and smash together to combine.
3. Finely shred 12 ounces cooked boneless chicken with your hands. Add the chicken and 4 ounces shredded Mexican blend cheese (about 1 cup) to the bowl and stir and mash to combine.
4. Heat an air fryer to 400°F. Meanwhile, assemble the taquitos.
5. OPTION 1: CORN TORTILLAS
6. Stack 5 of corn tortillas on a microwave-safe plate. Cover with a very damp paper towel and microwave until warmed through, 30 seconds. Assemble the taquitos on a work surface or cutting board: Coat 1 tortilla lightly with cooking spray (keep the remaining covered). Flip the tortilla over. Place 3 tablespoons of the filling across the lower half of the tortilla in a rough log shape that's about 1-inch wide. Starting at the bottom of the tortilla, roll tightly up and secure closed with a toothpick (it's okay if the tortilla cracks a little).
7. OPTION 2: FLOUR TORTILLAS
8. Assemble the taquitos on a work surface or cutting board: Coat 1 flour tortilla lightly with cooking spray. Flip the tortilla over. Place 3 tablespoons of the filling across the lower half of the tortilla in a rough log shape that's about 1-inch wide. Starting at the bottom of the tortilla, roll tightly up and secure closed with a toothpick.
9. Repeat assembling as many taquitos as will fit in the air fryer basket in a single layer with space around each one (corn tortillas will crack as they sit, so only assemble one batch at a time).
10. Place the taquitos seam-side down in the air fryer basket. Air fry until crisp and the ends are browned, 5 to 10 minutes (corn tortillas may take longer). Meanwhile, assemble the next batch of taquitos, making sure to start with warm corn tortillas.
11. Transfer the taquitos to a plate (or baking sheet if you want to keep them warm in a 200°F oven). Repeat air frying the remaining taquitos. Let cool for 2 minutes before removing the toothpicks and serving. Serve with toppings or dipping sauces as desired.

Notes:

1. Make ahead: The filling can be made up to 2 days ahead and refrigerated in an airtight container.
2. Storage: Leftovers can be refrigerated in an airtight container for up to 4 days. Reheat in a 325°F oven, flipping halfway through, until warmed through, 15 to 17 minutes total. Alternatively, reheat in an 400°F air fryer, flipping halfway through, until warmed through, 4 to 6 minutes total.

Air Fryer Sausage Crescent Cheese Balls

Servings: 42

Ingredients:
- 1 lb bulk spicy sausage
- 2 cups shredded sharp cheddar cheese (8 oz)
- 1/2 teaspoon dried rosemary leaves, crushed
- 1 can (8 oz) refrigerated Pillsbury™ Original Crescent Rolls (8 Count)
- 2 tablespoons all-purpose flour

Directions:
1. Cut three 8-inch rounds of cooking parchment paper. Place one round in bottom of air fryer basket. Spray with cooking spray.
2. In large bowl, mix sausage, cheese and rosemary; mix well using hands or spoon.
3. Unroll crescent dough on work surface; coat each side of dough with 1 tablespoon of the flour. Using pizza cutter or knife, cut dough into about 1/4-inch pieces. Mix crescent dough pieces into bowl of sausage mixture in small amounts until well blended.
4. Shape mixture into 42 (1 1/4-inch) balls. Place 14 of the sausage balls on parchment in air fryer basket. Refrigerate remaining balls until ready to bake.
5. Set air fryer to 400°F; cook 6 minutes. Remove basket from fryer; use tongs to carefully turn sausage balls over. Cook 3 to 6 minutes longer or until browned (at least 165°F) and dough is cooked through in centers.
6. Cover cooked sausage balls with foil to keep warm while baking remaining sausage balls. Repeat two times for remaining sausage balls and parchment paper rounds.

Air Fryer Mozzarella Sticks

Servings: 3-4 **Cooking Time:** 10-30 Mins.

Ingredients:
- 400g block mozzarella cucina
- 2 tbsp plain flour
- 1 tsp garlic granules
- 1 large free-range egg
- 40g/1½oz panko breadcrumbs
- olive oil cooking spray
- salt and freshly ground black pepper
- Recipe tips

Directions:
1. Cut the mozzarella into strips, roughly 5cm/⅝in wide, and pat dry using kitchen paper.
2. In a shallow dish, mix together the flour and the garlic granules. In another dish, beat the egg with a generous amount of salt and pepper. Spread the breadcrumbs in a third dish.
3. Roll the mozzarella strips in flour, then in egg, then in flour and egg again, to create a double coating. Make sure each piece is totally covered in flour each time; any gaps will cause the mozzarella sticks to leak in the air fryer. Coat well in the panko breadcrumbs.
4. Freeze for at least 30 minutes until solid.
5. Spray the bottom of the air fryer basket with olive oil spray and arrange a single layer of mozzarella sticks in the bottom. Spray the top of the mozzarella sticks with oil before air-frying for 10 minutes at 200C. Repeat until all the mozzarella sticks are cooked, keeping each batch warm, then serve immediately.

Notes:
1. Mozzarella cucina is a firm, low-moisture cooking mozzarella sold in a block. Often labelled as ideal for pizza, it is shrink-wrapped rather than packed in whey.
2. This recipe was tested working in two batches in a 3.2 litre/5½ pint basket air fryer; in a larger air fryer the sticks can be cooked in one batch. It is not suited to a model fitted with a stirring paddle.

Air Fryer Halloween Mummy Dogs

Servings: 8   **Cooking Time:** 9 Mins.

Ingredients:
- 8 oz. (227 g) refrigerated crescent dough or crescent dough sheets, see headnote
- 8 hot dogs
- mustard
- ketchup or hot sauce
- oil spray
- EQUIPMENT
- Air Fryer

Directions:
1. Unroll the crescent dough. Cut into 3/8"-1/2" (9mm-13mm) wide strips.
2. Pat the hot dogs dry (helps keep the dough from slipping around while rolling).
3. Wrap a couple pieces of dough around each hot dog to look like bandages. Criss-cross them occasionally and make sure to leave a separation of the bandages on one end for the face. Stretch the dough if needed. Word of Caution: Don't wrap too many layers on top of each other or else the underlying ones may not cook all the way. Repeat for the remaining dough and hot dogs.
4. Lightly spray the ends of the wrapped hot dogs with oil spray. Spray the air fryer basket with oil spray. Lay the wrapped hot dogs face-side up in the air fryer basket or tray, making sure the mummies aren't touching (cook in batches if needed).
5. Air Fry at 330°F (166°C) for 6 minutes. Gently wiggle to loosen from the baskets.
6. Air Fry at 330°F (166°C) for another 1-3 minutes or until crescent dough is golden, and cooked through.
7. Dot the face with mustard and ketchup (or hot sauce) for the eyes and any other desired facial features. Enjoy!

Air Fryer Pizza

Servings: 4   **Cooking Time:** 7 Mins.

Ingredients:
- 1/3 cup Mozzarella cheese shredded
- 12 inch pizza dough homemade or canned
- 1 teaspoon olive oil
- 3 Tablespoons pizza sauce
- 1/4 teaspoon basil freshly chopped

Directions:
1. Preheat the Air Fryer to 375° Fahrenheit (190°Celcius).
2. Prepare the Air Fryer basket with olive oil or nonstick cooking spray and a parchment paper liner to prevent the pizza from sticking.
3. Roll the pizza dough out on a floured surface. Make the dough similar to the size of your Air Fryer basket. Carefully transfer it to the air fryer, then brush lightly with a teaspoon of olive oil.
4. Spoon on a light layer of pizza sauce and sprinkle mozzarella cheese on top along with your favorite toppings.
5. Air fry pizza for 7 minutes at 370 degrees Fahrenheit until you see a golden brown crispy crust and the cheese has melted.
6. Top with extra basil, cheese, and red pepper flakes just before serving to add additional flavor.

Notes:
1. Using freshly shredded mozzarella cheese will keep the pizza from becoming too greasy and soggy. You can also use a ball of mozzarella cheese and place the slices on top! You can use pre-shredded, packaged cheese, but fresh works better for this recipe.
2. This recipe was made with a 5.8 qt basket style Cosori Air Fryer. All air fryers cook a little differently, so make sure to adjust the cooking time with this recipe if you're using a different air fryer.
3. You can add toppings like pepperoncini peppers, banana peppers, mushrooms, and more.

Toasted Ravioli

Servings: 6

Ingredients:

- 2 large eggs
- 1/2 c. milk
- 1 c. Italian bread crumbs
- 1/4 c. freshly grated Parmesan cheese, plus more for serving
- Kosher salt
- Freshly ground black pepper
- 1 lb. frozen ravioli
- Marinara, warmed (for serving)
- Vegetable oil, for frying
- Marinara, sauce for serving

Directions:

1. FOR FRYING:
2. Line a large baking sheet with parchment. In a shallow bowl, whisk together eggs and milk. In another shallow bowl, combine bread crumbs and Parmesan. Season with salt and pepper.
3. Working one at a time, dip ravioli in egg mixture then in bread crumbs, pressing to coat. Place on prepared baking sheet. Freeze until solid, 30 minutes.
4. In a large pot over medium heat, heat 2" oil until shimmering (about 365°). Working in batches, fry ravioli until golden and pasta is cooked through, 3 to 4 minutes, flipping as necessary. Place on a paper towel lined plate and immediately sprinkle with more Parmesan.
5. Serve warm with marinara for dipping.
6. FOR AIR FRYER:
7. Line a large baking sheet with parchment. In a shallow bowl, whisk together eggs and milk. In another shallow bowl, combine bread crumbs and Parmesan. Season with salt and pepper.
8. Working one at a time, dip ravioli in egg mixture then in bread crumbs, pressing to coat, then dip back in egg mixture. Place on prepared baking sheet. Freeze until solid, 30 minutes.
9. Working in batches, place in basket of air fryer and cook at 400° for 7 minutes. Remove from basket and top with Parmesan.
10. Serve warm with marinara sauce for dipping.

Air Fryer English Muffin Pizzas

Servings: 4   **Cooking Time:** 5 Mins.

Ingredients:
- 4 English muffins sliced in half, making 8 pieces
- ½ cup pizza sauce
- 1 cup mozzarella cheese shredded
- Optional Toppings: Such as pepperoni, mushrooms, ham, pineapple, olives, onions

Directions:
1. Air frying four muffin halves at a time, place muffins in the air fryer, cut side up. Air fry at 380 degrees F for 2-4 minutes, until slightly crispy.
2. Remove muffins from the air fryer. Spread about one tablespoon of sauce onto each muffin. Top with cheese and preferred toppings.
3. Return to the air fryer basket and air fry again at 380 degrees F for 3-5 minutes, until the cheese melts.

Notes:
1. Turn it into a breakfast pizza - Use a whole wheat muffin, add some sausage, sprinkle cheese, and add fresh basil on top. You can easily make this a fun breakfast pizza for the whole family.
2. Add veggies - You can easily add green peppers, fresh tomatoes, and more! I also love adding extra sauce as well! More toppings equal more sauce!

Air-fryer Jalapeño Poppers

 Servings: 4

Ingredients:

- 2 ounce cream cheese, softened
- ¼ cup finely chopped cooked chicken breast (about 1 1/4 oz.)
- ¼ cup finely shredded sharp Cheddar cheese (1 oz.)
- ¼ cup finely chopped green onion
- 2 tablespoon bottled cayenne pepper sauce (Frank's Red Hot®)
- 2 teaspoon chopped fresh dill
- 4 large jalapeño peppers, halved lengthwise (about 1 1/2 oz. each)
- 2 tablespoon whole-wheat panko breadcrumbs
- Nonstick cooking spray

Directions:

1. Combine cream cheese, chicken, Cheddar, green onions, hot sauce and dill in a medium bowl; stir until well combined. Clean seeds and membranes from jalapeños and stuff evenly with the cream cheese mixture. Sprinkle with breadcrumbs. Place the stuffed jalapeños in the basket of an air fryer; coat with cooking spray. Cook at 370°F until the tops are browned and the jalapeños are tender, about 10 minutes.

Air Fryer Sausage

Servings: 6　　**Cooking Time:** 8 Mins.

Ingredients:
- 6 thin Italian sausages Italian or standard
- 1 serving cooking spray

Directions:
1. Preheat the air fryer to 200C/400F.
2. Lightly pierce the sausages in 2 places, through their casing.
3. Lightly grease the air fryer basket, then add a single layer of sausages in it.
4. Air fry the sausage links for 8 minutes, or until fully cooked.

Notes:
1. TO STORE: Pu leftovers in airtight containers to store in the refrigerator for 3-4 days.
2. TO FREEZE: Use freezer safe bags or containers to freeze sausages for up to 6 months.
3. TO REHEAT: Reheat in the microwave for a few seconds or in the air fryer for 2-3 minutes.

VEGETABLE & & VEGETARIAN RECIPES

Crispy Air Fryer Brussels Sprouts

Servings: 4 **Cooking Time:** 15 Mins.

Ingredients:
- 1 pound Brussels sprouts
- 1 tablespoon olive oil
- 1/2 teaspoon kosher salt
- 1 medium shallot
- 2 tablespoons unsalted butter
- 1 teaspoon red wine vinegar

Directions:
1. Heat an air fryer to 375°F. Meanwhile, trim 1 pound Brussels sprouts and halve any that are larger than an inch wide. Transfer to a medium bowl, add 1 tablespoon olive oil and 1/2 teaspoon kosher salt, and toss to combine.
2. Add the Brussels sprouts to the air fryer and shake into a single layer. Air fry, stopping to shake the basket (or rotate the pans in larger air fryers) about halfway through, for 15 minutes total. Meanwhile, prepare the shallot butter.
3. Finely chop 1 medium shallot. Place 2 tablespoons unsalted butter in a medium microwave-safe bowl and melt in the microwave. (Alternatively, melt in a medium saucepan over low heat, then remove from the heat.) Add the shallots and 1 teaspoon red wine vinegar and stir to combine.
4. When the Brussels sprouts are ready, transfer into the bowl or saucepan with the shallot butter and toss to combine. Serve immediately.

Smokey Cheese & Caramelized Onion Potato Bake

Servings: 6-8 **Cooking Time: 1 Hour**

Ingredients:

- 1.2kgs potatoes (or enough when sliced to fill your dish)
- 1 onion
- 2 large leeks (or another onion)
- 1 cup cream
- 1/2 cup milk
- 1 1/2 tsp salt
- 1/4 tsp nutmeg
- 1 bay leaf (optional)
- ½ - ¾ cup smoked cheese

Directions:

1. Set your Instant Pot to Sauté mode and add the olive oil. Add the thinly sliced onions and leeks. Cook for 15 minutes on Less, stirring occasionally, until soft and lightly golden.
2. While the leeks and onions cook, peel and thinly slice the potatoes (1mm slices are the ideal thickness).
3. Before assembling your bake, check that your baking dish fits comfortably in your Instant Vortex. We used a round 21cm dish, that was 9cm deep.
4. Spoon your caramelized leeks and onions into the bottom of your round baking dish. Add roughly ☐ of your grated smoked cheese on top of this. Flatten the filling to form a nice base for the potatoes.
5. Arrange the potato slices vertically in your dish. Tuck any remaining potato slices into the gaps. Pop your bay leaf, in the middle between a few slices of potato.
6. Wipe down the inner pot, and then add the milk, cream, salt and nutmeg. Set to Sauté on Less (push button to change the setting) and let the mixture heat up until nearly boiling. Remove the inner pot carefully and then pour mixture over the potatoes. Scatter over the remaining cheese and cover the bake tightly in tin foil.
7. Start your Instant Vortex, set it to the Bake function at 180c for 50 minutes. Add the potato bake to the Vortex basket and cook until the potato slices are soft and cooked through. Ours was done at 45 minutes but we recommend checking from 40 minutes onwards, as cooking times will vary depending on how thick your potatoes are sliced, and your baking dish of choice.
8. Once the potatoes are cooked through. Remove the foil, and cook for a further 5-10 minutes, so that the top turns a deep golden brown.
9. Serve alongside your favourite main dish.

Air Fryer Squash

Servings: 2-4   **Cooking Time:** 20-25 Mins.

Ingredients:
- 2 medium or 1 large summer squash
- 2 medium or 1 large zucchini
- 1 teaspoon kosher salt, plus more as needed
- 1/2 teaspoon garlic powder
- 1/2 teaspoon Italian seasoning
- 1/4 teaspoon freshly ground black pepper, plusl more as needed
- 1 tablespoon olive oil
- 2 sprigs fresh basil, divided
- 1 small lemon

Directions:
1. Trim and cut 2 medium summer squash and 2 medium zucchini crosswise into 1/4-inch-thick rounds. Transfer to a colander set in the sink. Sprinkle with 1 teaspoon kosher salt and toss to coat. Let sit for 10 to 15 minutes to allow some moisture to release. Meanwhile, heat air fryer to 400°F.
2. Transfer the squash to a paper towel-lined baking sheet in a single layer. Thoroughly pat dry with more paper towels, then transfer to a bowl. Sprinkle with 1/2 teaspoon garlic powder, 1/2 teaspoon Italian seasoning, and 1/4 teaspoon black pepper. Drizzle with 1 tablespoon olive oil and toss to coat.
3. Transfer the rounds to air fryer basket. Air fry until golden at the edges, tossing the squash halfway through, 20 to 25 minutes total. Meanwhile, remove the leaves from 2 fresh basil sprigs and tear into pieces.
4. When the squash is ready, add about 2/3 of the basil to the basket and toss to coat. Taste the squash and season with kosher salt and black pepper as needed. Transfer to a medium serving bowl. Just before serving, finely grate the zest from 1/2 small lemon with a Microplane or the small holes of a box grater over the squash. Garnish with remaining basil leaves.

Notes:
1. Make ahead: Cut the squash up to 1 day ahead and refrigerate in airtight container or resealable bag.
2. Storage: Leftovers can be refrigerated in an airtight container up to 4 days.

Air-fryer Green Tomato Blt

Servings: 4   **Cooking Time:** 10 Mins.

Ingredients:

- 2 medium green tomatoes (about 10 ounces)
- 1/2 teaspoon salt
- 1/4 teaspoon pepper
- 1 large egg, beaten
- 1/4 cup all-purpose flour
- 1 cup panko bread crumbs
- Cooking spray
- 1/2 cup reduced-fat mayonnaise
- 2 green onions, finely chopped
- 1 teaspoon snipped fresh dill or 1/4 teaspoon dill weed
- 8 slices whole wheat bread, toasted
- 8 cooked center-cut bacon strips
- 4 Bibb or Boston lettuce leaves

Directions:

1. Preheat air fryer to 350°. Cut each tomato crosswise into 4 slices. Sprinkle with salt and pepper. Place egg, flour and bread crumbs in separate shallow bowls. Dip tomato slices in flour, shaking off excess, then dip into egg, and finally into bread crumb mixture, patting to help adhere.
2. In batches, arrange tomato slices in a single layer on greased tray in air-fryer basket; spritz with cooking spray. Cook until golden brown, 4-6 minutes. Turn; spritz with cooking spray. Cook until golden brown, 4-6 minutes longer.
3. Meanwhile, mix mayonnaise, green onions and dill. Layer each of 4 slices of bread with 2 bacon strips, 1 lettuce leaf and 2 tomato slices. Spread mayonnaise mixture over remaining slices of bread; place over top. Serve immediately.

Air Fryer Pickles

Servings: 4   **Cooking Time:** 8 Mins.

Ingredients:

- 2 cups dill pickle chips
- 1/4 cup white whole wheat flour
- 1 large egg
- 1 tablespoon water
- 1/3 cup whole wheat breadcrumbs
- 1/3 cup panko breadcrumbs
- 1 1/2 teaspoons paprika
- 1/2 teaspoon Italian seasoning
- 1/4 teaspoon kosher salt plus additional for serving
- 1/8 teaspoon cayenne pepper
- Greek Yogurt Ranch Dip optional for serving

Directions:

1. Spread the pickles out onto a clean kitchen towel or paper towels. Pat as dry as possible.
2. Set up your workstation: place the flour in a shallow bowl (a pie dish works well). In a separate shallow bowl, whisk the egg and water until well combined. In a third shallow bowl, combine the whole wheat breadcrumbs, panko breadcrumbs, paprika, Italian seasoning, cayenne, and salt. Arrange the plates in a line (flour, eggs, breadcrumbs). Line a large, rimmed baking sheet with parchment paper.
3. Working a few pickles at a time, dredge the pickles in the flour, then the egg, then the breadcrumbs, shaking off excess as needed.
4. Place on the prepared baking sheet. Repeat with remaining pickles.
5. Preheat your air fryer to 400 degrees F. Generously coat the basket with nonstick spray. Arrange a single layer of pickles in the basket so that they do not overlap. Coat the top of the pickles with nonstick spray.
6. Air fry for 8 to 10 minutes, until dark golden and crisp (these cook fairly evenly so no need to flip halfway through unless you are a stickler). Remove the air fried pickles to a serving plate and sprinkle with a pinch of kosher salt. Enjoy hot.

Notes:

1. TO STORE: Refrigerate pickles in an airtight storage container for up to 4 days.
2. TO REHEAT: Recrisp leftovers on a baking sheet in the oven at 350 degrees F.
3. TO FREEZE: Spread leftover pickles onto a baking sheet and freeze until solid. Transfer the frozen pickles to an airtight, freezer-safe storage container or ziptop bag for up to 3 months. Reheat from frozen.

Air Fryer Squash And Zucchini

Servings: 4 **Cooking Time:** 8 Mins.

Ingredients:
- 1 large zucchini
- 1 large yellow squash
- 2 tablespoons olive oil
- 1 teaspoon Italian seasoning
- ½ teaspoon garlic powder
- ¼ teaspoon kosher salt
- ¼ teaspoon black pepper

Directions:
1. Preheat the air fryer to 400F for 5 minutes.
2. Trim the ends off the squash and zucchini, quarter them lengthwise, then slice into 1-inch thick chunks.
3. Place the squash in a large bowl, drizzle with olive oil, and sprinkle on seasonings, then toss to coat.
4. Spread the veggies into a single layer in the air fryer basket. Air fry for 7-8 minutes, tossing the basket halfway through the cook time, or until tender-crisp.

Air Fryer Mushrooms

Servings: 4 **Cooking Time: 7 Mins.**

Ingredients:
- 16 ounces mushrooms rinsed and dried
- 3 tablespoons olive oil or melted butter
- 1 clove garlic or garlic powder
- 1/2 teaspoon salt
- 1/4 teaspoon black pepper

Directions:
1. To make this easy air fryer mushrooms recipe, start with clean mushrooms. Then with cold water, and give mushrooms a quick rinse to remove any dirt off residue. Pat them dry with paper towels.
2. Add ingredients to the bowl of mushrooms, and then toss to mix mushrooms with olive oil, or melted butter. Then, add in the garlic, salt and pepper. Toss until the mushrooms are well coated with the seasonings.
3. Transfer mushrooms to air fryer basket. Air fry at 400 degrees F for 5-7 minutes.
4. Season to taste. You can also top them with parmesan cheese, onion powder, or other favorite seasonings.

Notes:
1. There is no need to shake the basket during the cooking process.
2. I use a Cosori 5.8 quart basket style air fryer. Because air fryers are different, air frying cook time may vary. Add a couple of minutes to cooking time as needed.
3. Fresh garlic is always a favorite, but you can use garlic powder as a substitute.
4. If using a larger air fryer, you can cook all mushrooms at once. If using a smaller air fryer, do not over fill the basket. Work in batches of mushrooms if necessary.
5. Depending on what you are serving, and the type of mushrooms, you can cut mushrooms in half, or slices. You can leave them whole if they are small, or slice them to your preference. If using a larger mushroom, they may cook better if sliced.

Air-fryer Asian Bbq Cauliflower Wing Recipe

Servings: 4   Cooking Time: 15 Mins.

Ingredients:

- 1 head cauliflower medium
- 2 cups panko bread crumbs
- 3 eggs large
- Korean BBQ Sauce
- 1/4 cup hoisin sauce
- 1/3 cup honey
- 1 tbsp soy sauce
- 1 tbsp rice vinegar
- 1 tbsp ketchup
- 1 tsp sesame oil
- 1/4 tsp ground ginger
- 2 cloves garlic minced
- 1/4 cup water cold
- 2 tsp corn starch

Directions:

1. Preheat air-fryer or convection oven to 400 F
2. Wash and dry a medium head of cauliflower. Cut cauliflower crown bit-size pieces removing any stems.
3. In a small bowl add 3 large eggs beat. In a large bowl add 2 cups of panko bread crumbs. Dip each piece of cauliflower first in the egg mixture and then into the panko bread crumbs. Before adding each piece to the panko bread crumbs be sure to shake off any excess egg. Toss the cauliflower in the panko bread crumbs and then place on a wire rack that will sit on top of the baking sheet. Ensure the cauliflower pieces are not touching or crowded so there is room for air to fully circulate around each piece. Air-fry or bake for 15 minutes. If using a convection oven flip the cauliflower pieces halfway through cooking.
4. Meanwhile in a small pot over medium-high heat add 1/4 cup hoisin sauce, 1/3 cup honey, 1 tbsp soy sauce, 1 tbsp ketchup, 1 tbsp rice vinegar, 1 tsp sesame oil, 1/4 tsp ground ginger and 2 minced garlic cloves. Stir to combine and let come to a small boil.
5. In a small bowl add 1/4 cup of cold water and 2 tsp of cornstarch. Mix well until cornstarch has been fully dissolved. Pour into the BBQ sauce mixture and mix well. Reduce heat to medium and continue to simmer the sauce until it thickens. About 2-3 minutes.
6. Transfer the cooked cauliflower pieces to a large bowl ad add the sauce. Toss until each cauliflower wing is fully coated. Serve immediately.

Notes:

1. Store any uneaten cauliflower in a tightly sealed container in the fridge for up to 3 days. The bites will not stay crispy but can be eaten cold or reheated in the microwave or in the oven.
2. Top with toasted sesame seeds or chopped green onions.

Air Fryer Sweet And Sour Veggies

Servings: 2 **Cooking Time:** 15 Mins.

Ingredients:

- Sauce
- 1/3 cup honey
- 2 tablespoons orange juice
- 1 tablespoons soy sauce
- 1 teaspoon red chili sauce
- 2 tablespoons water
- ½ tablespoon cornstarch
- Cauliflower Rice
- 10 oz. bag frozen riced cauliflower we used Birds Eye Steamfresh Original
- 2 teaspoons soy sauce
- Pinch of salt
- Vegetables
- 10.8 oz. bag frozen broccoli cauliflower, and carrots (we used Birds Eye Steamfresh)
- 2 large eggs
- 3 tablespoons all purpose flour
- ½ tablespoon garlic powder
- Other Ingredients:
- 1 teaspoon white sesame seeds
- 2 tablespoons minced green onions

Directions:

1. Preheat the air fryer to 400°F and spray the air fryer basket or shelf with non-stick cooking spray. Remove all of the vegetables from the freezer and let them sit for a couple of minutes.
2. Next, place all the ingredients (except for the corn starch) for the sweet and sour sauce in a small saucepan.
3. Prepare the sauce: Whisk the ingredients for the sauce together and bring to a boil over high heat.
4. Turn the heat to low, let the sauce simmer while you prepare the slurry. In a small jar, whisk the corn starch with 2 tablespoons of water until combined. Pour the slurry into the sauce and whisk everything together until it thickens. Cover and remove the sauce from the heat.
5. Prepare the riced cauliflower: Pour the frozen riced cauliflower into the air fryer basket and be sure you break up any large frozen chunks. Drizzle the soy sauce and a pinch of salt over the riced cauliflower.
6. Toss and spray the riced cauliflower with non-stick cooking spray.
7. Fry the riced cauliflower at 400°F for 5 minutes, toss, and fry for another 5 minutes.
8. Pour the riced cauliflower into a bowl and cover with tin foil.
9. Prepare the vegetables: Crack the eggs into a large bowl and whisk.
10. Add the frozen broccoli, cauliflower and carrots to the bowl and toss the vegetables until they are covered in egg.
11. In a separate bowl, add the flour, garlic powder, salt, and whisk together. Sprinkle the flour mixture over the vegetables and toss until the vegetables are coated with flour.
12. Pour the vegetables into the air fryer, spray with non-stick cooking spray, and fry for 7 minutes. Toss the vegetables and fry for another 8 minutes.
13. Add the cooked vegetables to a bowl and add the sweet and sour sauce to the bowl. Toss until the vegetables are coated in sauce.
14. Serve the vegetables over the riced cauliflower and sprinkle with sesame seeds and green onions.

Air Fryer Jacket Potato

Servings: 1 **Cooking Time:** 40 Mins.

Ingredients:
- Baking potato (Maris Piper is a good choice)
- Oil and seasoning

Directions:
1. Scrub and wash each baking potato and pat dry with some kitchen roll. Pierce with a fork and add a little oil on the skin, rubbing it all over. Season with salt if required.
2. Place in the air fryer basket and cook at 200C/400F for 40 minutes. Check on it half way through and turn the potato over. If the potato skin is crisping up too quickly wrap it in some foil.
3. Check the potato is cooked through by piercing it with a fork - it should be soft on the inside.
4. When the potato is ready, slice it in half and top with your favourite jacket potato fillings.

SALADS & SIDE DISHES RECIPES

Air Fryer Burst Tomato Burrata Caprese Salad

Servings: 2   **Cooking Time:** 10 Mins.

Ingredients:
- Tomatoes
- 1 pint heirloom cherry tomatoes (halved)
- 4 large whole garlic cloves (slightly smashed)
- 1 teaspoon olive oil
- 1/4 teaspoon salt
- Salad
- 3 cups baby arugula
- 1 small whole Burrata cheese (4 ounces)
- 1 tablespoon balsamic glaze (I use Dellalo)
- 1/4 cup torn basil
- 2 ounces sliced rustic loaf (sliced)

Directions:
1. Place tomatoes, garlic, 1 teaspoon extra virgin oil, and 1/4 teaspoon each of the salt and pepper in a bowl and toss, transfer to the air fryer basket. Cook 400F 10 minutes, shaking.
2. Place arugula on a platter. Drain burrata and add to the arugula. Top with roasted tomatoes and drizzle any juices that accumulated. Top with balsamic glaze, basil, salt and pepper. Serve with bread.

Air Fryer Roasted Garlic

Servings: 3 **Cooking Time: 30 Mins.**

Ingredients:
- 3 bulbs garlic
- 2 tablespoons olive oil

Directions:
1. Preheat the air fryer to 380°F.
2. Cut the top ¼ of the garlic off so the cloves are exposed and drizzle with olive oil.
3. Wrap the garlic in foil and place in the air fryer basket.
4. Cook the garlic for 30-35 minutes or until it is tender and golden.
5. Remove the bulbs and gently squeeze each clove to remove it from the skins.

Notes:
1. You can use just one bulb of garlic if you'd prefer, I do more at once and then store extras in the freezer.
2. Once cooked open the foil and check the garlic, it should be very soft and lightly golden brown. Large bulbs may need a little bit of extra cooking time.
3. Roasted garlic can be used right from frozen, it softens quickly.
4. Keep leftover roasted garlic cloves in the bulb & cover them in the refrigerator for up to 1 week.
5. Freeze roasted garlic by squeezing out the cloves from the skins and then freezing them in a zip-top bag for up to 4 months.

Air Fryer Parmesan Brussel Sprouts

Servings: 4   **Cooking Time:** 12 Mins.

Ingredients:
- 1 pound brussel sprouts
- 1 tablespoon olive oil
- 2 cloves garlic pressed or minced
- 1/4 cup shredded parmesan cheese
- 1/4 teaspoon salt
- 1 pinch pepper

Directions:
1. Preheat the air fryer to 400 degrees
2. While the air fryer is preheating, cut the brussel sprouts in half and rinse.
3. Place the brussel sprouts in a large mixing bowl, and add in the olive oil and minced garlic. Toss the ingredients together until the brussel sprouts are coated.
4. Place the prepared brussel sprouts in the basket, and sprinkle salt and pepper on top.
5. Cook on 400 degrees Fahrenheit for about 10-12 minutes.
6. Sprinkle the parmesan cheese over the cooked brussel sprouts and return to the air fryer for one to two minutes, until melted.
7. Serve while warm.

Notes:
1. I use the Cosori air fryer, so start with ten minutes the first time you make this recipe, to avoid overcooking.
2. Weight Watchers: approx. 2-4 points
3. KETO: C/11 P/6 F/5

Sweet Potato Wedges With Cilantro Lime Crema

Servings: 6   **Cooking Time:** 22 Mins.

Ingredients:

- 4 medium garnet sweet potatoes
- 2 tablespoons olive oil
- 2 teaspoons kosher salt
- 1 teaspoon smoked paprika
- Cilantro Lime Crema:
- ½ cup Crema Mexicana or sour cream
- 1/3 cup fresh cilantro
- 3 limes, zested and juiced
- 1 teaspoon kosher salt
- Items Needed:
- Blender or food processor fitted with the blade attachment

Directions:

1. Cut the sweet potatoes in half crosswise, and then cut each half in half lengthwise. Slice the halves into ½-inch wide wedges, as evenly as possible, until all of the potatoes are cut.
2. Place the sweet potato wedges with the olive oil, kosher salt, and smoked paprika in a bowl and toss until the potatoes are evenly coated.
3. Select the Preheat function on the Air Fryer, adjust the temperature to 390°F, then press Start/Pause.
4. Place the sweet potato wedges into the preheated air fryer basket.
5. Set the temperature to 390°F and time to 22 minutes, then press Start/Pause.
6. Shake the basket halfway through the cooking time.
7. Combine the cilantro lime crema ingredients in a blender or a food processor fitted with the blade attachment and blend until smooth, then set aside.
8. Remove the sweet potato wedges when done and serve with the cilantro lime crema on the side.

Crispy Tofu With Palm Sugar Dressing In The Air Fryer

 Servings: 4   Cooking Time: 45 Mins.

Ingredients:

- 600 grams medium-firm tofu
- 2 bunches broccolini (700g), trimmed, thick stems halved lengthways
- 170 grams gai lan, trimmed, cut into 5cm lengths
- 3 egg whites
- 1 cup (180g) rice flour
- 2 tablespoons sesame seeds
- 1 tablespoon ground white pepper
- 2 teaspoons freshly ground black pepper
- 2 teaspoons salt
- olive oil cooking spray
- sliced green onions, sliced red chilli, extra sesame seeds and lime cheeks, to serve
- Palm sugar dressing
- 1 tablespoon finely grated ginger
- ¼ cup (60ml) extra virgin olive oil
- 2 tablespoons fresh lime juice
- ¼ cup (60ml) mirin
- ¼ cup (60ml) soy sauce
- 1 tablespoon finely grated palm sugar
- 1 small red chilli, chopped finely

Directions:

1. Cut tofu horizontally into four slices. Cut each slice in half to make eight pieces in total. Line a board with paper towel. Place tofu slices on paper towel; lay more paper towel on top of tofu, then top with a heavy tray (or small chopping board) to weigh the tofu down. Leave for 10 minutes to drain.
2. Preheat a 5.3-litre air fryer to 180°C for 3 minutes.
3. Rinse broccolini and gai lan. Taking care, pull out the air-fryer pan and basket; place damp vegetables in basket. Slide pan and basket back into appliance. Keep temperature set at 180°C; set timer for 5 minutes. Cook until vegetables are just tender. Transfer vegetables to a platter; cover to keep warm.
4. Meanwhile, make palm sugar dressing. Place ingredients in a screw-top jar; shake well to combine.
5. Beat egg whites in a shallow bowl. Combine rice flour, sesame seeds, peppers and salt in a second shallow bowl. Dip tofu slices in egg white, then coat in rice flour mixture; spray generously with oil.
6. Place half the coated tofu in basket. Keep temperature set at 180°C; set timer for 15 minutes. Cook, turning halfway through cooking time, or until tofu is crisp and golden. Transfer to a wire rack. Repeat with remaining coated tofu.
7. Top vegetables with crisp tofu, sliced green onion, sliced chilli and extra sesame seeds; drizzle with dressing. Serve with lime cheeks.

Air Fryer Italian Sausage With Peppers And Onions

Servings: 4　　　Cooking Time: 27 Mins.

Ingredients:

- 1 tablespoon oil
- 1 sweet pepper
- 1 small onion
- 4 Italian sausage links
- 4 sausage rolls, sliced down the middle

Directions:

1. Cut the sweet pepper into slices, removing the stem, seeds, and membranes.
2. Cut the top and bottom of the onion and remove the outside layer. Cut the onion in half and cut both halves into long slices.
3. Heat oil in an air fryer at 320 degrees for 1 minute in an air fryer sized pan.
4. Add peppers and onions into the pan and cook on 320 for 10-12 minutes, stirring occasionally.
5. Remove peppers and onions from air fryer.
6. Increase air fryer temperature to 380 degrees and add Italian sausage links.
7. Cook at 380 degrees for 10-12 minutes, moving basket halfway through to rotate.
8. Remove Italian sausages from the air fryer.
9. Assemble sausage links, peppers, and onions on the sausage rolls.
10. Place back in the air fryer at 380 degrees and cook for 1-2 minutes to crisp up the sausage roll.
11. Enjoy immediately.

Hummus-filled Portobellos With Olive Tapenade

Servings: 2

Ingredients:

- Hummus-Filled Portobellos:
- 2 portobello mushrooms
- 1 teaspoon olive oil
- 1 teaspoon kosher salt
- 1⅓ cups prepared hummus
- 1 teaspoon paprika
- Items Needed:
- Food processor fitted with blade attachment
- Olive Tapenade:
- 1 cup pitted kalamata olives
- ¼ cup olive oil
- 2 tablespoons capers, rinsed
- 2 tablespoons fresh parsley, chopped, plus more for garnish
- 2 garlic cloves, smashed
- 1 lemon, zested and juiced
- ½ tablespoon red wine vinegar
- ½ tablespoon fresh oregano
- ½ tablespoon fresh thyme
- Kosher salt, to taste
- Freshly ground black pepper, to taste

Directions:

1. Scrape out the gills underneath the mushrooms using a spoon and discard.
2. Brush the mushrooms caps with olive oil, then season with salt.
3. Fill each mushroom cap with hummus, then sprinkle paprika over the hummus.
4. Place the crisper plate into the Smart Air Fryer basket, then place the mushroom caps onto the crisper plate.
5. Select the Air Fry function, adjust temperature to 385°F and time to 12 minutes, then press Start/Pause.
6. Combine the olive tapenade ingredients in a food processor fitted with the blade attachment and blend until almost smooth, but some texture remains.
7. Season to taste with salt and pepper, then set aside.
8. Remove the mushroom caps when done.
9. Drizzle each mushroom cap with the olive tapenade, sprinkle with parsley, and serve.

Grilled Corn Salad

Servings: 4

Ingredients:

- 4 ears of corn, shucked
- 2 small poblano chiles
- 3 Mexican green onions
- 3 tablespoons (45 millilitres) olive oil, divided
- Kosher salt, to taste
- Black pepper, to taste
- 2 tablespoons (30 millilitres) fresh lime juice
- 1 teaspoon hot sauce (5 grams)
- 2 tablespoons (28 grams) fresh cilantro, chopped

Directions:

1. Place the cooking pot into the base of the Smart Indoor Grill, followed by the grill grate.
2. Select the Air Grill function on high heat, adjust time to 12 minutes, press Shake, then press Start/Pause to preheat.
3. Brush the corn, chilies, and onions with 1 tablespoon of oil and season to taste with salt and pepper.
4. Place the corn ears onto the preheated grill grate, then close the lid. Press Start/Pause to begin cooking.
5. Flip the corn ears over halfway through cooking. The Shake Reminder will let you know when.
6. Remove the corn ears and place the chiles and onions onto the grill grate.
7. Select the Air Grill function on high heat, adjust time to 8 minutes, press Shake, and press the Preheat button to bypass preheating. Press Start/Pause to begin cooking.
8. Turn the chilies and onions over halfway through cooking. The Shake Reminder will let you know when.
9. Remove the chilies and onions when done.
10. Cut the corn kernels from the corn ears and place in a large bowl.
11. Remove the seeds and stems from the chilies and chop into ½-inch pieces. Add to the bowl.
12. Remove the stems from the onions and chop into ½-inch pieces. Add to the bowl.
13. Whisk together the lime juice, hot sauce, and remaining olive oil in a bowl and pour over the grilled vegetables.
14. Add the cilantro to the vegetables and stir until everything is well incorporated. Season to taste with salt and pepper.
15. Serve immediately.

Air Fryer Salmon With Warm Potato Salad

Servings: 4   Cooking Time: 10-30 Mins.

Ingredients:

- 500g/1lb 2oz small new potatoes, larger ones halved
- 4 salmon fillets, approx. 150g/5½oz each, scaled
- 250g/9oz green beans (or thin-stemmed broccoli), trimmed
- 250g/9oz sugar snap peas (or mangetout)
- 1 long or 2 round shallots, finely chopped
- 2 tbsp white wine vinegar
- salt and freshly ground black pepper
- For the glaze
- 3 tbsp runny honey
- 3 tbsp wholegrain mustard

Directions:

1. Half-fill a large saucepan with water and bring to the boil. Preheat the air fryer to 200C.
2. Meanwhile, for the glaze, mix together the honey and mustard in a medium–large mixing bowl. Transfer half the glaze to a smaller container and season.
3. When the water is boiling, add the potatoes and cook for 7 minutes.
4. Line the air fryer basket with a piece of baking paper that covers the bottom and comes 2–4cm/about 1–1½in up the sides. Put the salmon, skin-side down, on the paper and brush the fillets with the seasoned honey-mustard glaze. (If you need to cook the salmon in two batches, use half the seasoned glaze per batch.) Air-fry for 6 minutes, then use a fork to check if the fish flakes in the thickest part; if not, cook for 1 minute more, or until cooked through.
5. When the potatoes have been boiling for 7 minutes, add the green beans and sugar snap peas and cook for a further 3–4 minutes, until everything is tender. If using mangetout, add only for the last 2 minutes of cooking time.
6. Drain the vegetables well. Stir the shallot, vinegar and some seasoning into the reserved honey-mustard glaze. Tip in the hot vegetables and gently stir to coat in the dressing.
7. Use the baking paper to help you lift the salmon from the air fryer and serve with the warm potato and vegetable salad.

Notes:

1. If you have a steamer basket, boil the potatoes in a pan for 10 minutes, then put the beans and sugar snaps in the basket above the boiling water and steam for the final 4 minutes. If using mangetout, steam for 2 minutes only.
2. For a romantic dinner for two, simply halve all the ingredients.

Air Fryer Vietnamese-style Spring Roll Salad

Servings: 4   **Cooking Time:** 20 Mins.

Ingredients:

- 340g vermicelli rice noodles
- 250g Coles Australian Pork Mince
- 1 garlic clove, crushed
- 2 tsp finely grated ginger
- 1 tsp lemongrass paste
- 2 tsp fish sauce
- 2 carrots, peeled, cut into long matchsticks
- 3 spring onions, thinly sliced lengthways
- 10 sheets spring roll pastry, thawed
- 1 cup (80g) bean sprouts
- 1/2 cup mint leaves
- 1/2 cup coriander leaves
- 2/3 cup (160ml) Vietnamese-style salad dressing
- 1 long red chilli, thinly sliced (optional)
- Select all ingredients

Directions:

1. Cook noodles in a large saucepan of boiling water for 4 mins or until tender. Refresh under cold water. Drain well. Cut 1 cup of the noodles into shorter lengths, reserving the remaining noodles.
2. Combine the cut noodles with the mince, garlic, ginger, lemongrass, fish sauce, half the carrot and one-third of the spring onion in a large bowl.
3. Place 1 pastry sheet on a clean work surface. Place 2 tbs of the mince mixture diagonally across 1 corner. Brush the opposite corner with a little water. Fold in sides and roll up to enclose the filling. Repeat with the remaining pastry sheets and mince mixture.
4. Preheat air fryer to 200°C. Spray spring rolls with olive oil spray. Place in the basket of the air fryer and cook, turning halfway through cooking, for 15 mins or until cooked through.
5. Meanwhile, divide reserved noodles evenly among serving bowls. Top with bean sprouts, mint, coriander and the remaining carrot and spring onion.
6. Cut the spring rolls in half and arrange over the noodle mixture. Drizzle with dressing and sprinkle with chilli, if using.

Notes:

1. On the stove: To make this without an air fryer, half-fill a small saucepan with oil. Heat over medium heat. Cook spring rolls, in batches, for 2 mins or until golden and cooked through. Cool slightly before cutting in half.

SANDWICHES & BURGERS RECIPES

Air Fryer Hamburgers Recipe

Servings: 4   **Cooking Time:** 12-15 Mins.

Ingredients:
- 3 slices thick-cut bacon (about 6 ounces, optional)
- 1 1/2 pounds ground beef, preferably 80% lean
- 2 teaspoons smoked paprika
- 1 tablespoon plus 1 1/2 teaspoons Worcestershire sauce
- Kosher salt
- Freshly ground black pepper
- 4 slices cheese, such as cheddar, pepper Jack, or Swiss (optional)
- FOR SERVING (OPTIONAL):
- Split hamburger buns
- Lettuce
- Sliced tomato
- Thinly sliced red onion

Directions:
1. Finely chop 3 slices thick-cut bacon, if using. Place in a medium skillet over medium heat and cook until the fat begins to turn semi-translucent, about 4 minutes. Transfer the bacon to a paper towel-lined plate.
2. Place the bacon, 1 1/2 pounds ground beef, 2 teaspoons smoked paprika, and 1 tablespoon plus 1 1/2 teaspoons Worcestershire sauce in a large bowl. Using your hands, quickly and gently mix until just combined.
3. Divide the mixture into 4 patties (about 6 ounces each). Season both sides generously with kosher salt and freshly ground black pepper.
4. Heat an air fryer to 380°F. Working in two batches if needed, place the patties in a single layer in the basket so that they are not touching. Air fry for 4 minutes. Flip the patties and air fry to desired doneness, 5 to 7 minutes more for medium. Top each patty with a slice of cheese, if using, during last minute of cooking. Serve in buns with toppings if desired.

Notes:
1. Make ahead: Form the patties and refrigerate in an airtight container with parchment or wax paper between each patty up to 2 days ahead before air frying. The patties can also be frozen up to 4 months. To cook from frozen, air fry at 350°F for 10 minutes. Increase the temperature to 380°F, flip the patties, and cook to desired doneness, 7 to 10 minutes more.
2. Storing: Air fryer burgers are best enjoyed right away. Leftovers can be refrigerated in an airtight container for up to 3 days.

Air-fryer Greek Turkey Burgers

Servings: 2

Ingredients:

- 8 ounce ground turkey breast
- 1 ½ tablespoon extra-virgin olive oil
- 2 teaspoon chopped fresh oregano
- ½ teaspoon crushed red pepper
- ¼ teaspoon salt
- 2 garlic cloves, grated
- ½ cup baby spinach leaves
- ¼ cup thinly sliced red onion
- ½ tablespoon red-wine vinegar
- ¼ cup crumbled feta cheese
- 2 whole-wheat burger buns, split and toasted

Directions:

1. Lightly coat air-fryer basket with cooking spray.
2. Combine turkey, oil, oregano, red pepper, salt and garlic in a bowl. Mix well. Form the mixture into 2 (1/2-inch-thick) patties. Place in the prepared air-fryer basket and cook at 360°F until a thermometer registers 155°F, 13 to 15 minutes, turning once during cooking.
3. Toss spinach, onion and vinegar together. Divide feta among top and bottom halves of buns. Place the burgers on the bottom halves of the buns. Top with the spinach mixture and the bun tops.

Air Fryer Frozen Beyond Burgers®

Servings: 2　　**Cooking Time:** 15 Mins.

Ingredients:

- 2 frozen Beyond Burger® patties , 1/4lb (113g) patties
- salt , to taste
- black pepper , to taste
- oil spray , for coating
- BURGER ASSEMBLY:
- 2 Buns
- Optional - cheese, pickles, lettuce, onion, tomato, avocado, cooked bacon etc.
- EQUIPMENT
- Air Fryer
- Instant Read Thermometer (optional)

Directions:

1. Spray or brush both sides of the frozen patties with oil and season with salt and pepper.
2. Spray air fryer basket or rack with oil. Place the frozen patties in the air fryer basket/tray in a single layer. Air Fry at 380°F/193°C for 8 minutes.
3. Flip the patties and continue cooking for about 3-6 minutes or until cooked through and internal temperature is 160°F/71°C. Timing will vary depending on thickness of patties and individual air fryer model.
4. For Cheeseburgers: add the slices of cheese on top of the cooked patties. Air fry at 380°F/193°C for about 30 seconds to 1 minute to melt the cheese.
5. Warm the buns in the air fryer at 380°F/193°C for about 1 minute.
6. Serve on buns, topped with your favorite burger toppings.

Air Fryer Bacon Cheeseburger Biscuit Bombs

Servings: 8

Ingredients:

- 1/2 lb ground beef (at least 80% lean)
- 1 teaspoon Montreal steak seasoning
- 1/2 cup chopped cooked bacon (6 slices)
- 1 can (16.3 oz) refrigerated Pillsbury™ Grands!™ Southern Homestyle Original Biscuits (8 Count)
- 4 slices (3/4 oz each) American cheese, cut in quarters
- Ketchup, mustard and pickle slices, if desired

Directions:

1. In 10-inch skillet, cook beef and steak seasoning over medium-high heat 5 to 6 minutes, stirring occasionally, until beef is brown; drain. Cool 5 minutes. Stir in bacon.
2. Separate dough into 8 biscuits. Press each biscuit into 5-inch round. Place 2 quartered pieces of American cheese into center of each round. Place about 1/4 cup beef mixture into center of each round. Gently fold edges up and over filling; pinch to seal.
3. Cut 8-inch round of cooking parchment paper. Place in bottom of air fryer basket. Spray with cooking spray. Place 4 biscuit bombs, seam sides down, onto parchment round in basket of air fryer, spacing apart.
4. Set air fryer to 320°F; cook 10 to 12 minutes or until biscuit tops are golden brown. With tongs, turn over each one; cook 4 to 5 minutes longer or until golden brown and cooked through. Remove from air fryer; cover loosely with foil to keep warm while cooking second batch. Repeat for remaining biscuit bombs. Cook as directed above. Serve with ketchup, mustard and pickles.

Air Fryer Hamburgers

Servings: 4 **Cooking Time:** 15 Mins.

Ingredients:
- 1 pound (450 grams) ground beef 80/20 mix of lean beef to fat must be kept cold
- 1 small (1 small) yellow onion finely diced
- 1 clove (1 clove) garlic minced
- 2 teaspoons (2 teaspoons) Worcestershire sauce
- Salt and pepper
- 4 (4) Buns

Directions:
1. Start by making the hamburger mix. In a mixing bowl, combine the ground beef with the garlic, onion, Worcestershire sauce, salt and pepper. Just fold in the other ingredients in the ground beef and make sure not to over mix the mixture.
2. Using your hands, quickly shape the hamburger patties and place on a tray. You want to make sure that the meat stays cold, because if you overwork the meat then the temperature of your hands will warm the meat up and that can result in really dense hamburgers. To shape the burgers, it's also a good idea to wet your hands a little as this will prevent the meat from sticking to your hands.
3. Preheat your air fryer to 395°F (200°C).
4. Lightly spray the air fryer basket with non-stick spray, and place your hamburger patties in the basket and cook to your desired doneness.
5. The best way to check for the doneness of the hamburger is by inserting a food thermometer in the center of the patty (see temperatures in notes below).
6. Now you're wondering how long are you going to air fry the hamburgers for. This depends on the thickness of your patties, but start with 12 minutes and keep checking until the hamburgers are cooking to your liking.
7. When the burgers are done, place cheese over each patty and the cheese will melt. This will result in a really delicious cheeseburger, and feel free to add more than just one slice of cheese if you like really 'cheesy' hamburgers just like my husband does!
8. Toast the buns in the air fryer on the same temperature, keep checking so that they're not burnt and just toasted.
9. Assemble the hamburgers and use your favorite toppings. I personally like mayonnaise, tomato slices, onion slices, and lettuce.

Notes:
1. Check the doneness of your hamburgers by inserting a cooking thermometer in the center of each patty:
2. Rare: 120-125f (52c)
3. Medium rare: 130-135f (57c)
4. Medium: 140-145f (63c)
5. Medium well: 150-155f (68c)
6. Well done: 160f (71c)
7. For gluten-free hamburgers, use gluten-free bread buns.

Halloumi Burger

Servings: 4   **Cooking Time:** 8 Mins.

Ingredients:

- 2 x 225g packs halloumi
- 1 x large carrot
- 50ml apple cider vinegar
- 1 x tsp caster sugar
- 1 x large vine tomato – thinly sliced
- 120g grilled peppers
- 1 x small baby gem lettuce
- 20ml olive oil
- 4 x tsp chilli sauce
- 1 x pack 4 Specially Selected seeded brioche buns
- Salt and black pepper

Directions:

1. Peel the carrot – then peel into ribbons.
2. Put the cider vinegar and sugar into a bowl, season with salt and pepper and add the carrot ribbons, marinate for 10 mins then strain off the liquid.
3. Quarter the lettuce, pull apart the leaves – wash and pat dry.
4. Drin the halloumi – cut each block into 4 slices.
5. Brush them with the olive oil.
6. Preheat the airfryer to 180°C.
7. Put the slices onto the fry basket – don't overlap.
8. Close the fry basket.
9. Cook for 8 mins.
10. Meanwhile split the buns and toast the cut sides.
11. Divide the lettuce leaves, grilled peppers, tomato and carrot strips, along with 2 slices of fried halloumi on the bases.
12. Drizzle with some chilli sauce then put on the tops and serve.

Fish Finger Sandwich

Servings: 4   **Cooking Time: 16 Mins.**

Ingredients:

- 2 teaspoons Dijon mustard
- 2 egg, whisked
- Flaked sea salt
- pepper to taste
- 75g golden crumbs
- 50g (15) Ritz Crackers, crushed
- 50g flour
- 500g uncooked cod, cut into finger sizes (2.5cm by 10cm)
- Cooking Spray
- 8 slices white bread
- Tartar sauce or ketchup
- Iceburg lettuce, shredded
- COOKING MODE
- When entering cooking mode - We will enable your screen to stay 'always on' to avoid any unnecessary interruptions whilst you cook!

Directions:

1. Place mustard, eggs and salt to taste in a shallow bowl, whisk together. Place crumbs and cracker crumbs in another shallow dish. Dredge each finger in flour, dip each fish finger in mustard egg mixture, then dredge in crumbs and proceed with all until are breaded.
2. Insert crisper plate in basket and basket in unit. Preheat unit by selecting AIR FRY, setting temperature to 180°C, and set time to 3 minutes. Press START/STOP to begin.
3. Select AIR FRY, set temperature to 180°C, and set time to 8 minutes. Select START/STOP to begin.
4. After 4 minutes, flip fish, spray other side and reinsert basket to resume cooking. Repeat until all fish fingers are cooked.
5. Spread tartar sauce or ketchup on one slice of bread, add lettuce and 3 fish fingers for each sandwich.

Halloumi Burger

Servings: 4   **Cooking Time:** 8 Mins.

Ingredients:

- 2 x 225g packs halloumi
- 1 x large carrot
- 50ml apple cider vinegar
- 1 x tsp caster sugar
- 1 x large vine tomato – thinly sliced
- 120g grilled peppers
- 1 x small baby gem lettuce
- 20ml olive oil
- 4 x tsp chilli sauce
- 1 x pack 4 Specially Selected seeded brioche buns
- Salt and black pepper

Directions:

1. Peel the carrot – then peel into ribbons.
2. Put the cider vinegar and sugar into a bowl, season with salt and pepper and add the carrot ribbons, marinate for 10 mins then strain off the liquid.
3. Quarter the lettuce, pull apart the leaves – wash and pat dry.
4. Drin the halloumi – cut each block into 4 slices.
5. Brush them with the olive oil.
6. Preheat the airfryer to 180°C.
7. Put the slices onto the fry basket – don't overlap.
8. Close the fry basket.
9. Cook for 8 mins.
10. Meanwhile split the buns and toast the cut sides.
11. Divide the lettuce leaves, grilled peppers, tomato and carrot strips, along with 2 slices of fried halloumi on the bases.
12. Drizzle with some chilli sauce then put on the tops and serve.

Fish Finger Sandwich

Servings: 4   **Cooking Time:** 16 Mins.

Ingredients:

- 2 teaspoons Dijon mustard
- 2 egg, whisked
- Flaked sea salt
- pepper to taste
- 75g golden crumbs
- 50g (15) Ritz Crackers, crushed
- 50g flour
- 500g uncooked cod, cut into finger sizes (2.5cm by 10cm)
- Cooking Spray
- 8 slices white bread
- Tartar sauce or ketchup
- Iceburg lettuce, shredded
- COOKING MODE
- When entering cooking mode - We will enable your screen to stay 'always on' to avoid any unnecessary interruptions whilst you cook!

Directions:

1. Place mustard, eggs and salt to taste in a shallow bowl, whisk together. Place crumbs and cracker crumbs in another shallow dish. Dredge each finger in flour, dip each fish finger in mustard egg mixture, then dredge in crumbs and proceed with all until are breaded.
2. Insert crisper plate in basket and basket in unit. Preheat unit by selecting AIR FRY, setting temperature to 180°C, and set time to 3 minutes. Press START/STOP to begin.
3. Select AIR FRY, set temperature to 180°C, and set time to 8 minutes. Select START/STOP to begin.
4. After 4 minutes, flip fish, spray other side and reinsert basket to resume cooking. Repeat until all fish fingers are cooked.
5. Spread tartar sauce or ketchup on one slice of bread, add lettuce and 3 fish fingers for each sandwich.

Air Fryer Turkey Burgers

Servings: 4   **Cooking Time:** 12 Mins.

Ingredients:
- 1 lb ground turkey
- 1/2 teaspoon salt
- 1/2 teaspoon pepper
- 1/4 teaspoon garlic powder
- 1/4 teaspoon smoked paprika
- 1 tablespoon olive oil
- 1 teaspoon Worcestershire sauce

Directions:
1. Add all the ingredients into a mixing bowl and mix well.
2. Lightly wet your hands and shape the mixture into four turkey burger patties.
3. Add the turkey burgers to a greased air fryer basket and air fry at 180C/350F for 12 minutes, flipping halfway through.
4. Let the burgers rest for 5 minutes before assembling them into burgers.

Notes:
1. TO STORE: Keep leftovers in the refrigerator, covered, for up to five days.
2. TO FREEZE: Place the cooked and cooled burgers in a shallow container and store them in the freezer for up to 6 months.
3. TO REHEAT: You can reheat turkey burgers for 4 to 5 minutes in your air fryer.

Air Fryer Butter Bacon Burgers

Servings: 2 **Cooking Time:** 17 Mins.

Ingredients:

- 1 pound lean ground beef
- 1 stick frozen butter, cut into small cubes
- ½ teaspoon salt
- ½ teaspoon freshly ground black pepper
- ½ teaspoon garlic powder
- 2 hamburger buns, split
- 2 slices bacon, cooked crisp
- lettuce, for serving
- red onion, sliced, for serving
- tomato, sliced, for serving
- ketchup, for serving
- mayonnaise, for serving

Directions:

1. In a large bowl, mix together beef, butter, salt, pepper, and garlic powder. Form mixture into 2 patties about 1 inch thick.
2. Spray both patties with oil and place in air fryer basket. Set temperature to 375 degrees, and air fry for 14 minutes, turning once, for medium rare. Remove burgers and keep warm.
3. Place hamburger buns in air fryer basket. Set temperature to 400 degrees, and toast for 3 minutes.
4. Sandwich each burger inside one toasted bun with 1 slice bacon, lettuce, onion, tomato, ketchup, and mayonnaise. Serve warm.

Low-carb Lettuce Wrap Burgers

Servings: 4

Ingredients:
- 1 pound ground beef
- 1½ teaspoons kosher salt
- 1 teaspoon black pepper
- 1 teaspoon onion powder
- 1 teaspoon garlic powder
- 1 teaspoon paprika
- 4 slices medium cheddar cheese
- 1 head Boston or butter lettuce, washed, root removed
- 1 Roma tomato, thinly sliced
- ¼ red onion, thinly sliced into rings
- ½ avocado, thinly sliced
- Ketchup, mustard, and mayo, for serving
- Items Needed
- Parchment paper, cut into 4 large squares

Directions:
1. Combine the ground beef, salt, pepper, onion powder, garlic powder, and paprika in a large bowl. Mix with your hands until just combined, being careful not to overwork the meat.
2. Divide the meat into four equal portions, shape each portion into a ball, then press into a patty.
3. Press down the center of each patty with your thumb to create a divot.
4. Remove the crisper plate from the Smart Air Fryer basket.
5. Place the beef patties directly into the air fryer basket.
6. Select the Air Fry function, adjust temperature to 380°F and time to 10 minutes, then press Start/Pause.
7. Place a slice of cheese on top of each patty.
8. Select the Air Fry function, adjust temperature to 390°F and time to 1 minute, then press Start/Pause.
9. Remove the burger patties when done.
10. Layer several lettuce leaves on top of each other to form 4 lettuce wraps.
11. Place each burger patty on top of a lettuce wrap.
12. Top the patties with tomato, onion, avocado, and condiments as desired.
13. Fold the lettuce wraps over the patties and toppings, then wrap the burgers with parchment paper halfway up the middle to hold the burgers together and serve.

Printed in Great Britain
by Amazon